MEN AND NATIONS

MEN AND NATIONS

BY

LOUIS J. HALLE

PRINCETON, NEW JERSEY

PRINCETON UNIVERSITY PRESS

1962

Copyright © 1962 by Princeton University Press

L.C. Card 62-10889

Louis J. Halle served in the U.S. Department of State, from 1941 to 1952 in the Office of American Republic Affairs and from 1952 to 1954 on the Policy Planning Staff. In 1954 he became a Research Professor in the Woodrow Wilson Department of Foreign Affairs at the University of Virginia, and in 1956 he accepted a professorship at the Institut Universitaire de Hautes Etudes Internationales in Geneva. He is the author of eight earlier books on foreign affairs and on his hobby, ornithology.

Publication of this book has been aided by the Ford Foundation program to support publication, through university presses, of work in the humanities and social sciences.

Printed in the United States of America by Princeton University Press, Princeton, New Jersey

TO THE MEMORY OF

ABRAHAM

WHO TOOK IT UPON HIMSELF

TO SPEAK TO THE LORD

PREFACE

Anyone who, trying to understand the practical questions of national policy, explores below the surface, discovers that they are rooted in questions of philosophy. For example, the answer to the question that confronted the prospective victors in World War II, whether to insist on the unconditional surrender of their opponents, ultimately depended on answers to questions about the nature of men and nations. If nations were corporate persons, some good by nature and others evil, and if the defeated nations were among the evil, then it might be a mistake to accept anything less than their unconditional surrender. But if nations were not persons, or if all shared a common nature, then reasons might appear why it would be wiser to negotiate terms.

This relationship between practice and philosophy explains why one who was professionally concerned with questions of policy came to be preoccupied, at last, with questions of philosophy. The book to which these remarks are prefatory is the final product of an investigation that began casually some ten years ago, when I was still in government, and has been pursued with mounting intensity up to this moment of its completion.

Originally, the book began with the practical questions. The form it took was that of an inquiry, pursuing the dialectical procedure of question and response down into the realms of philosophy. Each response would raise a further question, so that the process became self-propelling. One simply followed where the argument led. Sometimes it would lead to a dead end, in which case one would have to go back and look for an alternative line of advance. At last something like a final answer would begin to take shape. The inquirer who had spent years at the task would be tempted to believe that he was nearing its completion. Back along

vii

the line of the argument, however, there always remained unsatisfactorily resolved points—as he would bring himself to recognize at last. When he went back, then, and tried to deal with them, new insights would develop, illuminating new aspects of the problem. Perhaps an important addition to the vocabulary would be conceived. Then all was to do over again.

In effect, I sat down to write a philosophy before I had a philosophy, and developed one only in the process of thinking on paper. Once I had the philosophy substantially completed, however, I put aside all that I had written and made an entirely fresh start. Now my thinking was already done and I could begin with its conclusions. Instead of working my way from the questions to the philosophy that responded to them, I now began with the philosophy and proceeded to show its application. The result is one volume, less than half the length of its predecessors, into which much has been condensed. I cannot imagine that, in what remains of my life, I shall have anything essential to add.

Because my focus was on the problems of politics from the beginning, the book must be regarded as a work of political philosophy. But it is the application, rather than the philosophy itself, that deserves the adjective. The reader will see that, if I had begun my inquiry with questions concerning the nature of civilization, or with questions concerning the meaning of art, or with questions of religious experience, I would have arrived at the same philosophy. I would have arrived at it if I had set out, simply, to discover the meaning of life.

Since this is, however, a book of political philosophy, I should warn the reader against one possible disappointment. It does not—on the precedent of Plato, Hobbes, Rousseau, and others—offer a model of a political order regarded as final. What it does offer is an explanation of why such a model must be lacking.

In this final version I have undertaken to limit my text (Part One) to the essential argument. Only as much qualification and illustration as I have thought important for the understanding of that argument has been included with it. Since some statements, however, may appear dubious in a context so spare, the critical reader is occasionally bound to require more. I have therefore added in Part Two, entitled "Amplifications," what I should otherwise have felt obliged to include in the Text. Part Two also contains discussion of implications in the argument that, while not necessary to its understanding, are illuminating in themselves, and the sources of citations in the Text.

Thus organized, the book should serve the needs of two classes of readers. The reader who is content to know merely what the argument is will find Part One enough. The critical reader may refer, after each Section, to the supplementary material on that Section in Part Two.

Since, as now organized, each Section of Part One builds on the arguments of those that precede it, the only way to read it is from beginning to end. The reader who prefers simply to browse in a book, sampling a few Sections here and there, will, I am sorry to say, find himself frustrated if he attempts to do so here.

I ask the indulgence of the reader on one other matter. In such a structure of thought as I have tried to erect here, particular arguments are mutually interdependent; but they can be presented only one after another. It follows that arguments coming earlier may be inadequate pending refinement or correction in the light of arguments coming later. I therefore ask the reader not to render a final judgment until the structure has been set before him in its entirety.

It has long been evident that the philosophical consensus which supports civilization has broken down since the eighteenth century. The premises that once had general acceptance no longer provide a basis for mutual understanding among men and nations. I am not referring simply to the difference between our "Free World" and the "Communist World." The confusion prevails within our own world, within the world that calls itself free but is in doubt about the philosophical bases of freedom.

The lack of accepted and adequate premises makes the teaching of international politics, as of other subjects, a bewildering enterprise for teacher and student alike. The tacit and perhaps unpondered premises of one teacher may have nothing to do with those of the next. Propaganda terms get mixed up with the vocabulary of scholarship, mythological concepts are not distinguished as such, no two minds make the same identification of what constitutes reality. This alone may be justification for such an undertaking as this book represents.

No one in the twentieth century can be quite as pretentious about these matters as in earlier and more confident times. Perhaps I may nevertheless be allowed to say in conclusion, what Hobbes said of his masterwork: "There is nothing in this whole discourse . . . , as far as I can perceive, contrary either to the Word of God, or to good manners; or to the disturbance of the public tranquility. Therefore I think it may be profitably printed, and more profitably taught in the Universities, in case they also think so, to whom the judgment of the same belongeth."

L. J. H.

Geneva, 1961

CONTENTS

PART ONE: THE TEXT

CHAPTER I

THE DUAL PHILOSOPHY

SECTION I

THE THESIS of what follows is that we inhabit two worlds at once—like the performer in a circus who rides two horses, one foot on each. The disparity of the two worlds is the source of our main difficulties in the conduct of our individual lives and the organization of our societies.

I do not advance this as a personal discovery. It has been basic to philosophy and religion from primitive times, being set forth in the earliest writings that still survive, those of men who lived in Egypt more than five thousand years ago. The world's great religions are expressions of it. It is fundamental to the thought of such modern philosophers as Kant, Hegel, and Schopenhauer.

I shall try to show in these pages that past and present can be understood only in terms of this duality, and that the future must be approached in terms of it if the hope of human betterment is to be realized.

For most of us, the classic expression of the dual philosophy is identified with Socrates as Plato represented him. The two worlds of Socrates were the world of ideas and the world of material things. He took the view that only ideas are real, in the sense that they are elemental and eternal, while the multifarious concrete, individual representations of those ideas in the visible world are imperfect and transient reflections of them. The visible represents an attempt to copy the invisible, like an inferior artist's attempted reproduction of a great painting.

Flatly stated, this Platonic theory of ideas does not carry its own conviction. It can, however, be stated in terms within which, at least, it stands as a self-evident truth.

3

Let us ask: What is a straight line?

We may answer in either of two ways. We may say that a straight line is extension in one dimension and one direction only; or we may take a pencil and draw a straight line on a piece of paper. If, however, we give both of these answers, then we shall be faced with a discrepancy, for the straight line that we have drawn will not accord with the definition we have given. No matter how finely or how carefully we have drawn it, it will not be limited to one dimension (since material existence demands more than one dimension) and it will not be limited to one direction. It will have width as well as length; and the limitations of the materials that we used in drawing it, if not the limitations of our own control over them, will have resulted in some irregularities of direction, however slight. This discrepancy, between the definition and the example, demands reconciliation. How do we reconcile it?

We do it by distinguishing the idea from its concrete material expression. The concrete expression represents an effort to render the idea that, carried out within the natural limitations of the material world, can do no more than suggest it by approximating it as closely as possible. What was drawn on paper is not itself a straight line; it is merely suggestive of a straight line.

As a materialist I could proceed to say that only the line on paper has the value of what I call reality, while the conceptual line of the definition, having no material or measurable existence, is an illusion. I note, however, that in this case the conceptual line, the idea, assumes the fundamental role in the human mind. It is more "real" for the mind than the visible phenomenon. It comes first, since it was what we were trying to represent when we put pencil to paper. It also comes last, for when we look at what has been set on the paper our mind of its own accord eliminates as defects to be disregarded the width of the line and its irregularities of

4

direction. Our mind translates the visible, replacing it with the idea, which was the model by which the shape of the visible was determined. Therefore the idea, in the end as in the beginning, has the more vivid reality. The material phenomenon is only an imperfect imitation of it.

I have described the dualism, here, in particular terms. We can give it a general expression by identifying it with the two contrasting but interdependent terms, *perfection* and *imperfection.* Imperfection characterizes everything in the concrete world, thereby paradoxically associating the concrete world with the world of perfection, demonstrating the prior existence of the world of perfection. For how can imperfection be, except in terms of perfection? It is only by falling short of a standard of perfection in the mind that anything can be imperfect. In the very act of saying that a line is not perfectly straight we proclaim the existence of an idea, of the perfectly straight line that can have no material embodiment. It follows that the world of ideas is fundamental.

We accept the straight line as a concept of perfection that exists only in the imagination. We assume that the mark on the paper represents an attempt to imitate it with necessarily imperfect results. Suppose, however, that a critic of this reasoning should assert that the penciled line, while it might be regarded as an imperfect representation of the concept of one-dimensional extension in one direction, might better be regarded as a perfect representation of the concept of a shape that had just such length, just such width, and just such variations from straightness.

I reply that there is no such concept. The straight line, as we have defined it, presents itself to our minds as an elemental concept in nature, while the shape that corresponds exactly to the mark on the paper has no such standing. Everyone entertains the concept of a straight line; but that is not true of the putative concept of such a peculiar shape, which my mind could not hold to begin with (so that it was not in my mind when I set pencil to paper) or entertain even in looking at its perfect rendition. The one fits a universal pattern in our minds while the other does not. Therefore, when we look at the mark on the paper, what it evokes is the concept, not of a shape to which it corresponds exactly, but rather of a straight line, to which it does not correspond exactly.

Again, a circle exists in our minds as a natural concept. If, now, we are shown an object that has the shape of a circle except that its rim has been dented, that object will suggest the concept of a circle to us, and the deviation from circularity will present itself to our minds as an imperfection. The material object represents the concept of a circle imperfectly, rather than some other concept (that of its actual shape) perfectly.

What, in these examples of line and circle, is the basis of the distinction that impresses itself upon us between the true and the false claims to status as an elemental concept or idea?

The true concept has that regularity which makes it susceptible of expression in terms of a simple formula-definition. It represents a logic. The false lacks this quality. It represents no logic. There is no such formula to describe the exact shape of the mark which suggests a straight line as I found to describe a straight line itself, because it lacks regularity. It has features that do not occur according to any principle of logic. I can define a circle as a line extending in one plane and everywhere equidistant from a fixed point. But the distorted circle of my example, lacking regularity, is not susceptible of such definition.

I conclude that we have in our minds, as a matter of nature, a pattern of logical order that finds its expression in certain elemental concepts. When we look out at the concrete world we do so in terms of this pattern. We look for correspondences to it, and what we find, at best, are only approximations, correspondences that are more or less imperfect. Finding them, our vision strains to see in them the correspondences for which we are looking. It strains to correct the disorder, to assimilate it to the pattern of the ideal order which exists as a fact of nature in our minds. In the imperfection of the one world, consequently, we see the perfection of the other.

This raises the question of what the pattern of logic in our minds itself represents.

SECTION 2

In human creation the idea always comes first. The man who draws a straight line has the idea before he begins drawing. The sculptor has the idea of his statue before he addresses himself to the block of stone. When Robespierre assumed direction of the French Revolution he had an idea of the society which he meant to produce. No one undertakes any act of creation without a prior idea of what it is that he wants to create.

The dual philosophy assumes that what is true of human creation is true of all creation. The God of Genesis must have had the idea of light before he said, "Let there be light." There must have been an idea of man before there were men. There must, as well, have been a pattern of order outside the human mind before there was one inside. The one inside may, then, be supposed to correspond to the one outside. Thus, according to Socrates, the human idea of beauty corresponds to a truth of nature. It represents the human apprehension of what is divine. The sculptor who expresses it in a statue, although himself mortal, is expressing an eternal truth, a truth which existed before him and will remain after.

A duality in nature itself, independent of man, was the premise on which the artistic if not also the intellectual and political achievements of ancient Greece were based. When

Praxiteles fashioned his Hermes he was not taking an individual, physical man as his model; for every individual man was at best an imperfect copy of the original, the idea of man, and this original was his model; this was what he was trying to represent directly in stone.

The Platonic view has its theological expression in the untranslatable first five verses of the Gospel according to John, in what is called the doctrine of the *Logos*: the idea came first, and the idea came from God, and the idea was God. Christianity, as it was conceived by its founder, Paul, was rooted in this view. "We look not to the things that are seen," he wrote, "but to the things that are unseen; for the things that are seen are transient, but the things that are unseen are eternal."

Here, then, is a possible basis of more-than-human authority for the ideas expressed in human creation. The human creation expresses an idea in the mind of its creator that he supposes to reflect, in turn, the logic of the cosmos, the *Logos* that was in the beginning. The truth of the idea depends on its correspondence to the *Logos*.

At this point we encounter a basic epistemological difficulty, that of knowing whether anything in one's mind corresponds to anything outside it. The difficulty is that we cannot know what confidence to place in the organs through which we perceive and interpret what we suppose to lie outside. What seems blue to me might seem another color to someone with other eyes, and blue may not have any existence outside my mind. So, likewise, the logic that I attribute to the universe may be a property only of my own mind.

This difficulty must be accepted as a bar to certainty. When we have granted so much, however, it remains impossible in practice for us to believe that there is no correspondence at all between what we experience as reality and an actual reality outside. Those who pretend to believe so contradict themselves by their own actions, for they are bound to conduct their lives in terms of the external world whose existence they deny. The conduct of their lives, then, must be based on an unavowed philosophy more practical than the one they avow. It is such a practical philosophy that concerns us here.

We must assume, and dualistic philosophy does assume, some correspondence, however imperfect, between seeming and reality, between the pattern of order in our minds and the cosmic environment to which it seems to apply. One may be agnostic and still make assumptions on which to base the conduct of one's life.

At best, however, the correspondence which we assume between the world of ideas within and a world of ideas without must be imperfect. The ideas that present themselves to our minds cannot all be equally true by the test of such correspondence, if only because they conflict with one another. Nietzsche's idea of man does not agree with that of St. Francis, nor does Karl Marx's with that of St. Paul. So we face the problem of distinguishing truth from illusion, like a visionary who cannot tell whether a particular vision comes from God or Satan.

This is the human dilemma.

The thesis for which I contend at this point remains simple, without the elaborations that particular philosophies and religions have given it. We live in two worlds, a primary world of perfect ideas and an imperfect world which imitates it. We conduct our lives in accordance with the ideas as they present themselves to our minds. Because we cannot know how much truth there is in these ideas, however, we cannot agree on them.

SECTION 3

We live in both worlds at once, but it is the world of ideas that governs our bearing and conduct in the visible world.

9

Even where we are not consciously aware of it, we are ruled by our ideas of what is proper to mankind as a matter of nature or of God's intention, taking for granted both the *Logos* and the correspondence to it of these ruling ideas.

As individuals and as societies, however, we do not agree in our ideas of human propriety. Although we know what ways of life are proper to other species, we do not know what is proper to our own. The honeybee's way of life is not different today from what it was ten thousand years ago, or different on one continent from what it is on another. The osprey, too, has the same modes of behavior and association today that it had two thousand years ago when Pliny the Elder observed it at Ostia. No question can be raised about what is the proper way for these creatures to conduct their lives. The puzzle of propriety is exclusive to our own kind. It is only our own kind that has not yet established what it is, what life is proper to it, and what behavior. So we find it experimenting and going from one thing to another (often with disastrous results) as no other creature does.

It follows that anyone who tried to write a descriptive statement, like Maeterlinck's *The Life of the Bee*, of The Life of the Man would find himself faced with peculiar difficulties. Maeterlinck could study one community of honeybees and assume that his observations were valid for all communities. An apian New York would not differ from an apian Paris or Peking. The hive has long been standardized. Its political organization has been established as far back as human knowledge extends and is no longer in question. The roles of queen, drone, and worker are fixed, accepted, invariable.

But the society of the hive did not spring into being by one act of creation. Bees, as a species, evolved slowly from the same organic speck as man. Their first associations among themselves could not have manifested the elaborate and rigid organization we see today. (Rousseau might have said about bees what he said about men, that they were born free and are everywhere in chains.) There must have been variety and uncertainty in their social relations. Two communities would not be quite alike, and perhaps one would survive, perpetuating its kind, where the other would not. Among the varieties of organization, those best adapted to survival would become established while the others disappeared. The evolutionary process, based on natural selection, did not produce the individual bee only. It also achieved its completion in the modern hive, which no longer changes.

The history of human society, from the most primitive beginnings of which we know, has been one of constant variety in which no forms have become established. All is still experiment, change, breakdown, and renewed experiment. Typical nation-states of today, such as those of Western Europe, were unknown two centuries ago and may well have disappeared from the world of our grandchildren. The Soviet state today shows one kind of organization, the United States of America another, and both are in constant transformation. Neither is stable, neither established. One may speculate that this process of human evolution, of experiment and continuous change, will not go on forever but, like that of the bees in times past, is directed to an end.

The dilemma in which we men find ourselves today is that we cannot know what, if such is the prospect, that end will be; and so we cannot know in what direction we ought to move, to which of successive alternatives we ought to suit our minds and our wills. We cannot, in a word, identify what constitutes propriety for us. Any human observer is able to determine the behavior and the social organization proper to the honeybee; none can tell what is proper to himself.

> *The bee to the heather,*
> *The lark to the sky,*
> *The roe to the greenwood,*
> *And whither shall I?*

In the individual, the process of growing up is a process of discovering his individual identity, the kind of person he is to be and the way of life proper to such a person. In the species, the process of evolution has similar ends. That process has now been completed by every surviving species except man alone. "Man," says Sir Julian Huxley, "has now become the sole representative of life in that progressive aspect and its sole trustee for any progress in the future."

SECTION 4

The idea comes first and the life of man is an imitation of it. The sculptor who imitates in stone does not imitate in stone only. In the development of his own character, too, he imitates an idea of what a man should be. In the tone of his voice and the expression of his face, in his candor and in his reticences, in deciding when to take offense and when not to, in all these matters he is an actor playing a part.

No native of England is born with the idea of Englishman, but all are brought up to it. It comes to them from their accumulating experience of particular Englishmen, either directly or in accounts that are often idealized. It presents itself as an idea of propriety. (I recall an occasion in Geneva when a citizen, assuming that I was English, said to me: "*Vous n'avez pas le sang froid qu'on attend d'un gentleman anglais.*" I replied that I did not have to have it since I was an American.)

It is the primacy of the idea that gives importance to literary and artistic creation. Somewhere, Somerset Maugham has remarked that the Englishmen in Kipling's stories of India were more representative of the generation after he wrote than of that in which he wrote. There were Englishmen in India, a generation after, who would not have been what they were if he had not written them so. He not only created characters, Maugham concludes, he created men. In the beginning is the word.

12

The ideas by which men shape themselves are not, then, to be equated simply with the big doctrinal systems to which we give names: Democracy, Socialism, Platonism, Materialism, Existentialism, Taoism, Christianity. . . . They range from such formal systems down to ideas of men's clothing or the intonations of their speech. They range down to ideas of what the relations between the sexes should properly be. They range down to Mussolini's idea of man or Albert Schweitzer's idea of man, to Botticelli's idea of woman or Rubens' idea of woman. They involve the whole range of men's beliefs, attitudes, and behavior. And generally they are bound into complexes of ideas by association. (At one period in nineteenth-century France, Orleanists wore only side-whiskers, Bonapartists wore moustaches and goatees, while Republicans wore full beards.)

We men identify the ideas of propriety that each of us respectively entertains with the *Logos*, each of us basing his allegiance to them on the belief or assumption that they represent what is right in terms of what God or nature intended. "There is," says Cicero, ". . . a true law—namely right reason—which is in accordance with nature, applies to all men, and is unchangeable and eternal. . . . It will not lay down one rule at Rome and another at Athens, nor will it be one rule today and another tomorrow. But there will be one law, eternal and unchangeable, binding at all times upon all peoples. . . . The man who will not obey it will abandon his better self, and, in denying the true nature of a man, will thereby suffer the severest penalties." Cicero identified his own views of human propriety with this natural law on the assumption that the logic of his own mind was the "right reason" which corresponded to it. The difficulty is that the logic of other men's minds has represented "right reason" otherwise, thereby arriving at other views of human propriety. The *Logos* itself may be the same

13

at Rome as at Athens, tomorrow as today; but the identification of it by the men of Rome has been different from the identification of it by the men of Athens, and the identification made by the men of one age has been abandoned in favor of another identification by the men of the next.

This experience suggests that, unlike Cicero, we should distinguish between the ideas that we have in our minds and the *Logos* itself. The *Logos* remains largely unknown: the ideas in our minds represent only our partial apprehension of it, or our supposition of what it must be. The idea of the Athenian (as described in Pericles's funeral oration), the idea of the Roman (as represented by Cincinnatus at the plow), the old Teutonic idea of man as a warrior, the Quaker idea of the peaceable man—each of these may, by comparison with others, have points of greater and points of lesser correspondence to the original idea (i.e., the *Logos*). But they are not the original idea itself.

The dual philosophy holds that, implicit in the order of nature from the beginning, there has been an idea of man that represents what he is intended to be. We ought to model ourselves on it, as Cicero and others have affirmed. But we are able to apprehend it uncertainly at best and cannot agree on it. In our ignorance and disagreement, then, some of us follow Nietzsche and some St. Francis, some Kipling and some Gandhi, some Tolstoy and some Hitler. Without knowledge of the ultimate, we are constrained to make do among conflicting opinions as best we can.

The discrepancy of the rival ideas provokes conflict among their respective followers. The conflicts, however, are not simply conflicts among individuals, for no individual lives in intellectual isolation. Rather, each shares common ideas of propriety with his neighbors, who have attended the same schools and been taught the same lessons. He forms a community with them by virtue of this sharing.

14

Does not every community, then, represent a complex of ideas that distinguishes it from other communities representing other complexes of ideas, so that the conflict among ideas takes the form of conflict among communities?

We have now reached a point from which our path takes us out, for a while, over ground beset by philosophical quagmires. Up to this point we have been dealing with the visible individual and his individual mind. Now, however, we are to deal with the community and what we call the common mind. Although we habitually talk of the community as if it had an existence as tangible as that of the individual, we shall find that it does not.

CHAPTER II

THE PHILOSOPHY AND THE COMMUNITY

SECTION 5

"ALTHOUGH we speak of communities as of sentient beings; although we ascribe to them happiness and misery, desires, interests, and passions; nothing really exists or feels but *individuals*."

If we accepted Dr. Paley's statement simply, taking it in its literal sense, would it not follow that the record of human history was the chronicle of what did not really exist? Would it not follow that the history of France, for example, was the history of an imaginary entity? Presumably, however, he was thinking at the moment in terms of the visible world only, the world of concrete and sentient beings, and this was what he meant by real existence.

The visible world, however, would be unintelligible if one could not group its component particles, if there were no valid associations to be made among them. Intelligible experience depends on that process of generalization and synthesis in which we indulge when the individual molecules, in their association, are seen by us as constituting a blade of grass, and when the blades of grass are seen as constituting a green field. The pattern of logic which is native to our minds embraces such association, and sanity depends on it.

Associations among the concrete particles which we experience, however, are of different kinds, and are valid in varying degrees. The molecules that make up the blade of grass are associated by common organization in a single organic structure. That is one kind of association. The blades of grass that make up the green field are associated by their likeness to one another. That is another kind of association.

In so far as France is an organized state, its citizens, however diverse they may be, are associated by organization. In so far as France is a nation, they are associated by likeness—the same race, the same language, allegiance to a set of ideas that constitute a common culture, etc.

Associations by likeness, however, are matters of more or less. When I refer to the green field I am making a generalization that associates its particles by a common color. But the field may contain occasional blue and yellow flowers, a sprinkling of fallen brown leaves, or the grey stalk of last year's thistle. My generalization, then, is not absolutely true. It is, rather, a simplification which eliminates the exceptions, pretending that they are not there. The more prominent the exceptions, the less true my generalization would be; and no one can say how much less true it could become before it had become untrue.

The individual blade of grass is not a matter of more or less, but the green field is. The human individual is not a matter of more or less, but the human community is.

A community may differ from an individual in another respect as well. There can be no question about the physical boundaries of the individual man, where he leaves off and the world outside him begins. But there may be a question about the boundaries of the community.

My reference to the green field assumes, not only the association of its particles by a common color, but also their collective distinction from what lies immediately outside their community. I assume a field with absolute boundaries distinguishing it from its surroundings.

Such an assumption, however, may also represent a compromise with truth. Perhaps the field merges gradually into stony desert on one side, into woodland on the other, and should be regarded as part of a continuum between them; so that one cannot say, except arbitrarily, where it begins and where it leaves off. And perhaps this putative field is itself so variegated within any boundaries one might draw as to raise a doubt whether the differences within are not as great as any contrast with what lies without. Consequently, the tacit assumption that the green field exists, its tacit identification as an entity suitable for generalization, may again be only more-or-less true.

If the French people and the neighboring German people merge into each other (as perhaps they could be said to do, for example, in Alsace), and if the differences within each of these nominally distinct entities approach in magnitude the differences between them, then the question arises how much truth there is in the assumption of their distinct existence. Perhaps one could with equal truth divide the total area occupied by German and French people into a dozen nominal entities; or one could identify that area as a single entity, rather than two, on the basis of a contrast with its surroundings which exceeds any differences within.

The existence of the individual is absolute and unmistakable. There is no gradation between his existence and his nonexistence, and no doubt about his boundaries. A community, on the other hand, is a matter of degree. There are marginal cases in which one must remain uncertain whether an aggregation of individuals could be said to constitute a community at all.

Community is a categorical noun which we apply to uncategorical associations, thereby making them conform in concept to our logic. It eliminates the uncertainties that belong to an association in the process of giving it expression. This nominal imposition on the reality is compounded by our disposition to refer to communities as if they were corporate persons. But the metaphor of the corporate person would be more relevant if it evoked the image of ghosts rather than of solid persons. For nothing prevents two or more communities from occupying the same space at the same time, from containing one another or from overlapping. The corporate person differs from the individual person in that any of its constituent particles may belong to more than one such person at a time. The particle (you or I) may belong to a family, a tribe, a city, a race, a nation, or a species; it may belong to a political party, a church, a bureaucracy, or a trade. It may belong simultaneously to several or all of these. Corporate persons, then, like so many phantoms, may occupy the same space at the same time by virtue of sharing the same particles; and sometimes (as in the case of the family, which ramifies indefinitely) they are without outline, so that it is hard to know where they leave off. Since history is made (and then written) in terms of corporate persons, this peculiar and incorporeal character could be said to account for much of the intellectual confusion that has always attended both the unfolding of history and its interpretation.

When we think of the individual as a constituent particle of a corporate person, then the question arises: what corporate person? Is the corporate person mankind—as in the doctrine of original sin? Is it Islam, or Christendom? Is it the nation, the state, the city, or the parish? Is it the immediate family, or the family to the fourth generation—in which case would each of us belong simultaneously to several families? Is it a church, or a political party, or a monastery? Was Socrates a European, a Greek, or an Athenian? Was Paul a member of the tribe of Benjamin, a Jew, a Christian, or a Roman? What is a Jew? (The immigration authorities of the new state of Israel, which has decided to admit for settlement all who are Jews and only those who are Jews, now faces the practical problem of finding an answer to this last question.) In a book at my hand I come upon a reference to "the mind of Asia." Farther on I find an account of the attitude of the Orient toward the Occident. What correspondence is there between this distinction and another I had been reading about, the distinction between the attitude of the Old World and that of the New World?

The history of mankind is the record of these conflicts and confusions of corporate persons, all interlocked and entangled with one another, constantly forming and dissolving, separating and merging. It is the record of concepts of reality in the mind to which the realities themselves correspond more or less imperfectly. It is the record of bewildered individual persons caught up and involved in the consequent contradictions, struggles, and disasters.

SECTION 6

In the existential world, as Paley noted, only individuals really exist. Does it not follow that their associations must belong, rather, to the world of ideas? If, in the existential world, there are Frenchmen but no French nation, does it not follow that the French nation must be an idea?

We have observed that, in terms of the dual philosophy, ideas are primary, the phenomena of the visible world being created in imitation of them. Now, however, we face a paradox. For it is clear that generalizations are derived from the existential reality, to which they must therefore be secondary. The generalization of the green field is derived from the visible green of the individual blades of grass. The generalization which is the French nation is presumably derived from a physically manifested quality of likeness among Frenchmen. Here the existential reality comes first.

How do we resolve this paradox?

We must begin by asking whether a generalization is, in fact, an idea in the sense in which we used the term when setting forth the dual philosophy.

I would contend that a generalization is, in the first instance, nothing more than a device of logic that serves the purpose of economy. The story-teller in *The Arabian Nights*, having to practice the opposite of economy—being called upon, that is, to tell a story that would last forever in the telling—began by relating how first one ant entered the granary and made off with one grain of wheat, then another entered and made off with another grain of wheat, and so on. The repetitious action was matched by repetition in the telling to put off the moment when the telling would be over. But if the usual considerations of economy had prevailed the story-teller would have resorted to generalization, saying in one sentence that the army of ants entered the granary and made off with the store of wheat.

In describing what I call the green field I might, likewise, refer consecutively to each blade of grass and say that it is green. As a matter of economy, however, I reduce the entire description to one phrase by the device of generalization.

We have now defined a generalization as ("in the first instance") merely a logical device. But it is as hard to separate the device from the concept it conveys as to separate words from their meanings. The generalization that the grass is green conveys to my mind a concept of the grass. I shall therefore say, if only as a matter of convenience, that a generalization is a concept of existential realities that pretends to represent them as they are.

Now let us return to our problem of distinguishing between a generalization and an idea. Let us distinguish, in the example we have taken, between the concept of the blades of grass as they actually are and the idea that preceded their existence as the idea of the straight line preceded the pencil-mark on the paper. We say that there was an idea of green before there were blades of grass to embody it, and that the color of the blades is in imitation of that idea. The green was in the idea; it is in the multiple individual blades that are derived from the idea; and it is in the generalization that

I have, in turn, derived from the observation of the individual blades.

We must bear in mind, here, the relationship between the one and the many. There is only one idea of a straight line, but there is no limit to the number of pencil-marks that may be made in imitation of it. A generalization reduces the many to one again.

Although both the idea and the generalization are singular, by contrast with the plural phenomena which are derived from the one and which lead to the other, they are different in their essential character. Thus the idea from which the plural reality is derived is distinguished by its perfection from the generalization of that reality.

For example, we may suppose that the observation of particular women led the sculptor of the Aphrodite of Melos to apprehend, by retracing the direction of creation, that idea of woman which he was undertaking to express in his statue. His statue, then, represents the idea. In New York, in the American Museum of Natural History, there is another statue of a woman which represents something else. Its form and dimensions correspond to averages derived from measurements made of a large series of actual American women about twenty years old. It is presented as a composite or average of the young women of America, and consequently as being typical. It is, in other words, a generalization based on the scientific observation of the plural reality from which it is derived. The contrast between it and the Aphrodite is the contrast between the imperfect existential world, on the one hand, and a vision of the perfect world on the other. It is the contrast between generalization and idea.

However, while the two are fundamentally different, a generalization may resemble an idea superficially, as the statue of the American woman resembles the Aphrodite of Melos. Both have a simplicity that the existential reality itself lacks. The process of generalization, in reducing the many

22

to one for the sake of economy, is a process of simplification. It cannot accommodate exceptions, as the reference to the green field cannot accommodate the exceptions represented by the blue flowers or the brown leaves. A generalization, therefore, is a concept of what things are actually like that misrepresents them to the extent that it replaces their variety by a unity that they do not actually have. Pretending to represent what actually is, it presents, rather, a simplified version of what is.

An idea has this same simplicity. Variety is only in the imperfection of existential things, and the idea in the human mind does not pretend to represent them. What it pretends to represent is the one perfect model, of which they are the variegated copies. There can be no variety to the idea of the straight line, which is singular; variety belongs only to the plural imitations of it in the existential world.

Generalization and idea, in the simplicity which they share, may bear a superficial resemblance to each other that causes confusion between them. The idea of green, imitated in the blades of grass, may not differ clearly from the generalization of the green observed in those same blades of grass. The difference between the statue of the American woman and the Aphrodite may not seem as fundamental as, in fact, it is. The human mind, which cannot accommodate the complexity of the existential world, takes refuge in a simpler picture, whether that picture represents an idea or a generalization. Where circumstances allow, it is prone to confuse the two.

The man who generalizes about the green field has the entire subject of his generalization within the range of his physical vision, so that he can see the exceptions with his own eyes. This makes for an element of discipline in observation. But the man who generalizes about the French people is dealing with what lies beyond the scope of his vision. He is therefore less able and less likely to discipline in himself

23

the tendency to confuse an idea, which is always more vivid and appealing, with a generalization. He is the more apt to present an ideal vision of the Frenchman, and to present it in the guise of a generalization from the plural reality, which it is not.

This accounts for a paradox that anyone may test for himself. My reference to the green field might be borne out by actual measurements which would show that green, while not the only color present, was overwhelmingly predominant. Take anyone's description of "the typical Frenchman," however, and then travel about the French countryside, about the French cities and towns, trying to match it in flesh-and-blood. Anyone who makes this test must be impressed, in the end, not only by the individual variety that he finds among the French people, but by the scarcity of individuals who are in any substantial degree representative of the image regarded as typical.

This image of "the typical Frenchman" is not, as it pretends to be, a generalization derived from the existential reality, from the world of visible things. The man who entertains it is like an observer who, after examining thousands of lopsided circles, presents the perfect circle as typical of them. What has happened is that, by observations made in the visible world (and, we may be sure, by exposure to a literary tradition as well), he has been led to the apprehension of an image from the world of ideas which he has equated with the existential reality—which he has, in fact, substituted for it in the guise of generalization.

In so far as this same image is entertained by the people inside France, as well as by those outside, it represents a creative idea that they are drawn to imitate. As such, then, it is primary rather than derivative.

The French nation is not really a generalization derived from the existential reality but, rather, an idea by which the existential reality is molded.

Every community, in the degree to which it is coherent, represents an idea (or, better, a complex of ideas) that defines it and makes possible the conception of it as a corporate person. The concept of France has such a basis, and the question whether a majority of individual Frenchmen embody it is irrelevant. The idea of Frenchman represents the way the French picture themselves, and the way we picture them, rather than the way they are. That idea is expressed in French history, not necessarily as it actually happened, but as it is taught to French school-children for the purpose of perpetuating the idea. It is represented by the national heroes, the national literature, and the national art. But it is not necessarily realized in any large degree by the majority of living Frenchmen.

Perhaps the idea alone can give the community the singleness and integrity which we attribute to it when we think of it as a corporate person. But different communities are the bearers of different ideas. The rivalry and conflict among ideas, then, expresses itself in rivalry and conflict among communities. Frenchmen, perhaps, see the prevalence over their German neighbors of an idea of man or society inimical to their own, an idea which may even represent a direct threat to them if it has the effect of impelling the Germans to make it prevail beyond the borders of their own country. (The Germans, for their part, might want to make it prevail beyond the borders of their own country in order to forestall the prevalence of the French idea which seems threatening to them.)

If, then, Germany presents itself to the minds of Frenchmen as that abstraction, a corporate person—and as a corporate person representing an alien species—perhaps their justification is in an idea of the German that exists not only in the French minds but that also exists in German minds and molds them, determining the actions of the German nation. It is not enough to dismiss the idea by saying that only a minority of Germans substantially embody it in their own persons.

At this point we may well pause to clarify a distinction that has been emerging in the course of our argument.

The thesis of these chapters is that we live in two real worlds at once, a world of ideas and a world of material things. Both worlds are real in the sense that they exist independently of us and are not merely our imaginings. On the other hand, ideas of propriety and generalizations represent, respectively, our imaginings of what the two worlds of reality are.

We formulate these ideas of propriety and these generalizations in words—or in symbols that correspond to words. This is to say that they dwell in our minds as names and are nominal concepts (e.g., the idea of "decency" is a nominal concept, the idea of "the Frenchman" is a nominal concept, the generalization of "the Frenchman" is a nominal concept). In addition, then, to saying that we inhabit two worlds of reality, we may also say that we inhabit, at one and the same time, a real world and a nominal world. We inhabit the real world in an ultimate sense, the nominal world in a proximate sense.

SECTION 7

We have just said that each community may be defined by its ruling idea, whether or not the existential reality represents it closely. We have pictured the community as made up, perhaps, of widely varying individuals, but unified by a common idea of propriety which all alike are drawn to imitate. One community is thus distinguished from another, and the conflict of ideas therefore takes the form of conflict between communities.

But this, too, is a gross simplification. For the battle-lines in the conflict of ideas do not ordinarily coincide with the boundaries of formally defined communities. The conflict goes on between the great organized communities and within them as well; it goes on among and within the smaller communities inside the larger; it goes on among individuals within communities, whether in public debate, in after-dinner conversation, or in arguments between adolescent children and their parents (between the younger generation and the older, with their opposed concepts of propriety); and, finally, it goes on in the form of those inner conflicts to which all individuals are subject.

There is, in Germany, more than just one idea of the German. There is the idea of the German as a kindly, beer-drinking, music-loving, pipe-smoking, *gemütlich* family man. There is the idea of the German as the poetical or mystical philosopher, living in a world of abstractions, like Goethe's Faust. There is the idea of the German as a martinet with cropped hair, scarred face, and monocle, ruling the world by his superior discipline and will-power. Germany is the scene of an inner conflict among these ideas, with one tending to be predominant at one time, another at another time. Hitler's significance is that he represented a particular idea of the German which he managed to make predominant for a decade. It was not a new idea, and with Hitler's downfall it did not perish, but it was only one of several competing ideas to which the Germans were brought up.

In Italy, Mussolini tried to realize the idea of the Italian as a warrior and failed. In Japan, the idea of the Japanese as a lover of landscapes and flower-arrangements has vied with the idea of the Japanese as a ruthless warlord.

There is in the United States an idea of the American, widely held, that includes traits of physiognomy as well as of behavior and attitude. The physical characteristics of Negroes do not allow them to conform to this idea, so that their presence as an important element of the community constitutes an obstacle to its realization. Those who are possessed by the idea, then, feel that animus against Negroes which we call racial prejudice. The reason why sexual relations or intermarriage between Negroes and whites arouses particular passion among them is that it implies the future proliferation of Americans who do not conform to the idea which they are seeking to imitate. But this idea of Americanism comes into conflict, within the American community, with other ideas of Americanism that do not exclude Negroes, ideas that are, indeed, inimical to such exclusion.

What distinguishes German Jews from other Germans, perhaps, is simply an idea of Jewishness. This alone, a notion in the mind, is what makes them Jews. Then a Hitler comes along with an idea of Germanness for which he seeks a monopolistic predominance. The idea of Jewishness stands in the way and must be removed. The real conflict, here, is not between races (it is not clear that the Jews are a race) and not even directly between opposed ways of living. It is between opposed ideas. But Hitler's idea of Germanism, which excluded the Jews, was an issue inside Germany as well as outside, so that an appreciable measure of force and intimidation was necessary to make it prevail.

In addition to such differences within, there are similarities without. The traditional idea of the Englishman's social reserve, representative only of a certain social class in England, may be observed among members of the same class in Boston, Stockholm, or Zürich no less than in London. Here we see manifested, again, the ghostlike character of corporate persons, who can overlap one another, occupying the same space at the same time.

All this has to be simplified and categorized in the human mind, which abhors uncertainties and complexity. The mind, especially where it is not subject to the corrective of worldly experience, tends to equate each community with a single abstraction in the form of a generalization. When I was a child I lived altogether in the land of such abstractions. In

28

that land all Chinamen wore pigtails, walked with mincing steps, bowed repeatedly, and expressed themselves in repetitive and high-pitched musical monosyllables; all Englishmen were aristocrats; all Germans (it was the time of the First World War) were ponderous and self-assertive brutes; all Italians were day-laborers filled with song and vitality.

When the generalization with which the mind equates the community seems noble, then the community is identified with virtue—as in the manifestations of nationalism. When it seems alien and evil, then the community is seen as an alien and evil species.

Communities are associations based on ideas. We think of them in these terms, simplifying the existential reality. In fact, however, these associations are constantly threatened by internal disagreement, by the conflict of ideas that goes on inside as well as among them.

CHAPTER III

THE PHILOSOPHY, THE COMMUNITY, AND THE STATE

SECTION 8

WE MEN, challenged by the disparity of the two worlds we inhabit, respond by trying to make the existential world conform to the world of ideas, in our thoughts or in actuality. Looking at the mark left by the pencil, we see in it the perfect line that it is not. Or we try to reform it, erasing the grosser imperfections, doing it over. We are similarly moved to make the existential reality of diverse individuals conform to the idea of the community.

In Section 5 we noted that there are two kinds of association, represented in human society by the community and the state. The community is an association by likeness, the state by formal organization. The community, which exists as a matter of degree, and the state, which exists categorically, interact on each other.

The community, as it develops, is impelled to seek its more perfect realization in the state. For only the state can lend it that categorical definition which it otherwise lacks. The state has boundaries which become the boundaries of the community, and by pretending to speak for all its members the state enacts the idea that the community has one mind.

The reverse process also occurs. Where the state already exists it is moved to promote the development of a corresponding community within its jurisdiction; since, in the absence of a community with which to identify itself, it may not be able to command the acceptance of those whom it attempts to rule. For it is the community, rather than the state by itself, that draws men's allegiance.

Community and state, then, invoke each other.

Since the community is the more primitive, having some foundation in nature, we think of it as coming first; while we think of the state, which represents the imposition of artificial form on the natural substance of the community, as coming second. In historical fact, however, the state often comes first and summons the community into being *ex post facto.*

The community, as a nominal idea, may owe its generation and existence to a name alone. Give a name to a community that does not exist and the community will come into existence as a consequence. For example, if one should divide a group of school-children at random into two teams, naming them "The Rangers" and "The Bulldogs," the members of each would quickly come to cultivate, as a matter of pride, their collective distinction from the members of the other. Each would acquire distinctive characteristics, as a community, that it had not had to begin with. "The Bulldogs" might come to manifest those qualities of stubbornness which they associated with the animal of their name, while "The Rangers" came to be distinguished by their speed and agility. The name defines the idea, which the existential reality, in turn, imitates. In the beginning is the word.

Under its former Spanish rule, Central America was all one colony with one name. The withdrawal of that rule was followed by a period of anarchy in which various adventurers tried to capture, for themselves, as much of the territory as they could. The outcome was five holdings that correspond to the five Central American republics of today. What each represents is the limited area over which one man, in circumstances of chronic disorder, was able to extend his personal rule. If Nicaraguans think of themselves as one nation today, and Hondurans think of themselves as another, and Salvadorans as still another, that is because, like the school-chil-

31

dren, they have accepted what was nominal as real, and have imitated it.

In this example the state came first; it took on a name, a flag, and other symbols of community; and finally, by the power of nominal suggestion, the community itself came into being. Nicaraguans are Nicaraguans, not by any original distinction in nature, but because, being so named in the first instance, they have learned to think of themselves as such.

In the last century efforts were made to unify Germany— that is, to bring together the host of separate German states into one national state corresponding to what was conceived to be one national community. These efforts failed. The most that could be achieved was the creation of two German states, one to the southeast, the other extending from it to the North Sea and the Baltic. Although the two might have been called North Germany and South Germany, they were in fact called Germany and Austria. Up to the date of this settlement, no one had doubted that the Austrians were as much a part of the German nation as the Prussians, the Bavarians, the Saxons, and the rest. After the settlement, however, the nominal situation became determinative, so that Hitler's incorporation of Austria in the German state, sixty-five years later, was regarded as a violation by Germany of the separate Austrian nationality.

Today, as an aftermath of the Second World War, there are two Germanies instead of one. The international community has been perplexed by the problem of overcoming what everyone who was brought up in pre-war days has regarded as the abnormal division of the single German community into a West German and an East German state. But this formal division, given time, will at last impress itself upon the reality, altering the concepts of community. A new generation will arise to which it seems normal, and to which any amalgamation of the two Germanies would seem in violation of their identities as separate communities. (This process, however, would be more rapid if both states did not have "Germany" in their names.)

The state provides a nucleus upon which the idea grows, and the idea, in turn, shapes the existential reality.

SECTION 9

The community is an association by likeness, the state by common organization. Just as the cells of my body are organized into a physical entity, within which they are interdependent, so it may be said that individual men are organized into a state. "This great Leviathan, which is called the State," wrote Hobbes, "is a work of art; it is an artificial man made for the protection and salvation of the natural man...."

We must not be misled by the metaphor. The state, unlike the human body, does not belong to the visible world. Examples of the natural man can be seen and touched, but no one has ever seen or touched an example of Hobbes's artificial man. No one has seen a state; for the state is a nominal idea that manifests itself only in the compulsions to which it subjects the visible world. Like the invisible wind that bends the trees, we see it only in the effects it produces. Individual men act out the idea. But, although they act in the name of the state, they are not the state. Like iron filings in a magnetic field, by their disposition and movement they reveal, at second hand, an invisible pattern from the nominal world. Their role is that of the pencil which imitates the straight line.

In the organization of the hive the bees also enact an idea. The unalterable pattern of their behavior, however, demonstrates that the idea to which they respond represents a fixed finality. If it once was involved in a shifting conflict of ideas, that conflict has long been resolved. Today the idea stands without alternative, the ultimate realization of what must be regarded, for the bees, as their natural propriety.

Mankind, by contrast, has not yet apprehended the idea that represents its own natural propriety.

The question implicit in political theory from the beginning has been: What is the political organization proper to man as a matter of nature? To Aristotle it had been the city-state; to Dante and Thomas Aquinas it had been the universal empire.

The political theorists of the seventeenth and eighteenth centuries, however, abandoned the notion of a natural organization altogether. They took as the premise of their thinking the proposition that political organization, while necessary, is always artificial rather than natural. From Hobbes to Rousseau, they postulated a state of nature from which mankind had departed when it undertook to establish governments and the rule of law.

The artificial character of political organization explains human experience. We cannot simply dispense with organization on the grounds that we do not know what kind is proper for us. We have to establish a political order of some kind because otherwise we should live in that state of anarchy in which the arts of civilization have no chance to develop. But, whatever order we establish, it is a makeshift order. It is, at best, opposed to our nature as the order of the honeybees is not opposed to their nature. The day may come when we complete our evolution by some natural ordering of our society, but in our own time we have to make the best of the fact that it is not yet here. For us, the state of nature still lies in the future.

This poses the practical problem of investing any particular order for which popular acceptance is sought, artificial as it must be, with that appearance of natural or divine authority on which popular acceptance depends. The order must seem to represent, for men, the unique propriety that the hive represents for bees. This, in turn, requires a setting of legend. As truth may be told in fable, so the nomi-

34

nal idea of the political order is clothed in myth. (The myth of social contract, which Rousseau recognized as such, is one example. The Marxist interpretation of history is another.) Every political system depends for its support, then, on an accompanying mythology of its own. This mythology is associated particularly with the idea of sovereignty.

In every organized society there must be a sovereign from whom decisions flow, whether that sovereign is a man or an abstraction. The sovereign must appear before the subjects of sovereignty as if endowed with supreme authority. But nature, which has not provided mankind with the prescription of an organized society, has also failed to provide it with an authorized sovereign. It has made all men alike, stamping none with any caste-mark. In the artificial societies with which we have to make do, then, the bases of sovereign authority must be provided by legend. The divine right of kings is an example.

The old and established nation-states of the modern world assumed much their present shapes before it could be said of them that they were nation-states. As so many fragments ensuing upon the break-up of the universal mediaeval empire, they tended each to represent the area over which a feudal ruler was able to extend his sway. The boundaries of the English state represented the area that English kings were able to hold after they had failed to hold their continental possessions and to subdue Scotland. The boundaries of the French state represented the area over which the French kings were able to master the feudal barons and from which they were able to exclude rival potentates.

The classical states of modern Europe, then, first appeared as dynastic territorial possessions. England was the dynastic inheritance of Henry VIII, France the dynastic inheritance of Francis I. According to the prevailing theory, which they were able to realize to the extent that they were strong enough to do so, such rulers exercised a rule unlimited by any elements within their states; they claimed their authority by divine right and held themselves answerable to God only. The masses of people who lived on their territories and owed them allegiance were politically inert and obedient.

Under these circumstances there was no problem of locating the mind and will of the state, conceived as a personal entity. The locus of power, authority, and responsibility was in one physical person. When Louis XIV ordered his professional armies into the territory of France's neighbors, that was not the action of the French people. When the treaty ending Louis' wars was drawn up at Utrecht in 1713, nothing was said in it about "we the people of the United Kingdom" or "we the people of France." It was made, rather, between "the most Serene and most Potent Princess Anne, by the Grace of God, Queen of Great Britain, France and Ireland, and the most Serene and most Potent Prince Lewis the XIVth, the most Christian King."

This period of the divine right of kings is separated from our times by the revolution throughout Western civilization of which the French Revolution is the classic expression. That revolution took place in England by stages over a century and a half, beginning in 1688 if not earlier. It took place in the American colonies in 1776. It alternated with various forms of counter-revolution in France from 1789 to 1871. It did not occur in Russia until 1917, in Germany until 1918.

The actions of those who made the revolution responded to the idea of a nominal entity called "the people" in which sovereignty was vested by nature. The purpose of the revolution was to replace the rule of kings, conceived to be illegitimate, by the rule of this entity, which was conceived to be legitimate. But immediately the revolution took place an element of intellectual uncertainty and confusion was introduced which has played an incalculable part in statecraft ever since. For, if we say that an individual physical person is the ruler of the state and that the state represents his will, we are dealing in definable terms. We can isolate and identify the individual in question. We can see him; we can lay hands upon him; we can hear his voice. But what is "the people"— conceived as an entity that can take up the scepter which has been wrested from the king's grasp? No one has ever actually seen such an entity or heard its voice. If one wished to know what the will of Louis XIV was, one could go and ask him. If one wishes to know what "the will of the people" is, the problem is less simple.

What the revolution did was to take the authority of the state out of the hands of a physical person in order to confer it upon something that exists only as a concept in the mind. Having taken the scepter from the hands of the king, the makers of the revolution confronted the problem of putting it into the hands of "the people." Where was "the people"? Whose were the hands of "the people"?

Ever since the revolution this equivocation in logic on which it was based has constituted the prime dilemma of political theory. The theorists have all had to go on the assumption that the new sovereign, no less than the old, is a reality of the existential world, that it can exercise authority in a manner not altogether different from that in which the king once exercised authority, that it can make choices, and that there is a "voice of the people" by which it can make those choices known. The very terms on which political theory has been asked to base itself, then, have required it to be unreal by the test of literal truth, unreal in terms of the existential world.

What has happened is that the power of the state, taken away from actual kings, has come to be wielded, not by an actual entity called "the people," but by individual persons of flesh-and-blood who claim to be acting for such an entity— in its name, on its behalf, for its good, and perhaps with its assent. Just as the king claimed that he ruled with the authority of God (who is invisible and whose will has not been directly communicated to ordinary men), so the modern ruler claims that he acts with the authority of "the people" (which also is invisible and does not speak directly to ordinary men). For God and "the people" alike, whether they are nominal or real, belong to the world of ideas and not to the existential world.

Today, when the Premier of the Soviet Union addresses a communication to the President of the United States he undertakes to express the view of "the Soviet people" on the matter in question. When the President of the United States replies he gives the answer of "the American people" to the contents of the Premier's note. At San Francisco in 1945 sixty individual persons, vested with the authority of as many sovereign states, some of them what we call dictatorships and a few what we call liberal democracies, drew up and agreed upon a document that begins: "We, the peoples of the United Nations. . . ."

Granted that references to "the people" as a corporate entity with a corporate will are expressions of a concept from the world of ideas, the problem remains of establishing a relationship between what they represent and the world of flesh-and-blood. The state operates in both worlds and must find a correspondence between the idea on which it is based and the existential reality over which it holds sway. What is that correspondence?

SECTION 10

We conceive of communities as corporate persons, speaking of them "as of sentient beings," ascribing to them "happiness and misery, desires, interests, and passions." It is in these terms that we speak of those communities which we call "peoples." When we attribute sovereignty to the people we are thinking of the people as a corporate person that, like any individual person, is endowed with faculties for discharging the responsibility.

The chief such faculty is will, the faculty that defines personality. Each person is defined by a single will, each acts in response to that will. It follows that a corporate person, like an individual person, is defined by a single will, and that the exercise by the people of its sovereignty must respond to the guidance of such a will. So it is, at least, in the realm of ideas, if not in the existential world for which it supplies the models. "The Sovereign," wrote Rousseau, ". . . is but a collective being," and sovereignty is but "the exercise of the general will."

What is this general will?

The term "general" suggests that it represents a generalization, and generalizations, as we saw in the case of the green field, may be more or less true. If the inhabitants of a besieged city were on the verge of starvation their response to an offer of food might represent a unanimity which we would be fully justified in identifying as a general will. In reporting this we might list the names of the inhabitants, saying after each that he was in favor of accepting the offer. But we would mislead no one if, resorting to an economy of logic, we said that the response of "the people" was "yes." The statement does not have the literal truth attributable to a statement that the governor of the city responded; it represents some processing of the existential reality for ready assimilation by the mind; but, although one stage removed from literal truth, it is an accurate enough representation of that truth.

We can say, then, that the validity of the concept of a general will is repeatedly demonstrated by the contingent realization of substantial unanimity in human society. On any issue with respect to which the component individuals of a community are "of one mind," and where each one by his testimony gives evidence of such unanimity, one individual alone can truly represent the whole. If I have two

39

business partners, the three of us may explicitly authorize an agent to represent us and speak for us in making a certain proposal to an outsider. Within the limits of what we have authorized him to say, he can then truly claim to speak for our community of three as a corporate person with a corporate will.

Suppose, now, that our community consists of a hundred individuals, of whom one dissents from the position unanimously taken by the other ninety-nine. If we are quite literal we shall say, then, that the agent speaks for ninety-nine percent of the membership but not for the community as a whole. The lone dissenter, however, may not wish to appear intransigeant and to antagonize the rest of the group. He may therefore say that he will accept the majority opinion even though he thinks it wrong. He will agree in a nominal though not in a real sense. He will consent to have the agent overlook his individual dissent and speak for the group as a whole.

At this point, then, the literal truth becomes adulterated, however slightly, by the admixture of a conventional and agreed-upon fiction—a pretense. Everyone has agreed on a generalization that comes close enough to the truth even though it is not identical with the truth in detail.

In the example I have cited the conventional and fictitious element may be regarded as negligible. It is less negligible if twenty-five percent of the group dissents but finds that it is governed by a convention which assigns a value of zero to that dissent. It may become disturbing when conventional usage assigns a value of zero to forty-nine percent. Here the fiction is wide of the truth.

Let us take an historical example that has been much debated in our time. The question is whether Hitler was brought into power by the German people and was therefore representative of it, or whether he simply usurped power. Those who argue that he did represent the people are able to cite the fact that the National Socialist Party of which he was the head won an "overwhelming" victory in the Reichstag elections of 1933. It received more than twice as many votes as its nearest competitor, the figures being 43.9% for the National Socialists, 18.3% for the Social Democrats. To the question whether the German people did or did not favor the National Socialists the only answer that can be made with literal accuracy is that 43.9% of those who voted did, 56.1% did not. But convention has so impressed itself on our minds that we commonly accept this result as evidence that Hitler came into power in response to "the will of the German people"—even though this means assigning a value of zero to 56.1% of the votes plus an unknown portion of the abstentions.

The question whether we should regard a certain percentage of votes as representing the whole is not a question of what is the real truth. It is a question of what we should accept as nominally true. It is a question of what fiction we should adopt as a convention.

What has happened in the above example is that a concrete reality has been processed in men's minds, has been compounded with certain accepted fictions in accordance with the conventional procedure in all such cases, and the simple generalization which has been derived from this process has been put in place of the existential reality. The same thing happens when the President of the United States speaks for "the American people."

The acceptance of the conventional fictions that are here compounded with the facts is the way in which some of us have met the dilemma that confronts us when we undertake to place the power and authority of the state in the hands of a nominal idea, an abstract concept which exists only in our minds. Others have met it differently. When the Premier of the Soviet Union speaks for "the people" he does not rest his authority to do so on their suffrage. He rests it, rather, on a logic whereby he claims to have *a priori* knowledge of the general will.

What is this logic?

SECTION 11

The community, the state, the people—all these belong to the world of ideas rather than the existential world. The existential world seeks to imitate them but falls short of their perfection, just as the pencil-mark misses the perfection of the straight line.

Does not the "general will," as Rousseau termed it, also belong to the world of ideas?

Surely, if the community does, so does it, for it is no more than an attribute of the community. We have already seen in Section 6 that the element of likeness that makes the French people a community is a complex of ideas which Frenchmen share, rather than a generalization of the existential reality—although it might happen to correspond, in some respects at least, to such a generalization. The will of the French nation, in itself or in particular manifestations, is a part of that complex.

In the last section, however, we have been dealing with the general will as a generalization derived from existential reality rather than as an idea independent of existential reality. We have fallen back into the confusion that we had already picked our way through in Section 6, the confusion between an idea and a generalization.

If the community called France is an idea which the existential reality imitates, and if the fact that the majority of Frenchmen have hardly realized it in themselves is irrelevant to its validity, then we can also say that "the will of France" is an idea, and that a failure of the majority of individual Frenchmen to share it would be equally irrelevant. Winston Churchill may have represented "the will of Britain" better in 1945 than that majority of British voters who sent him out of office. Charles de Gaulle, throughout the 1940's, may have embodied the idea of France, and therefore "the will of France," whatever a majority of Frenchmen thought. If this is so, then the process of voting may be beside the point.

Rousseau, who was at home in the world of ideas as he was not in the existential world, was most reluctant to sacrifice the former to the latter by subjecting it to the test of a majority vote. A majority vote might go directly against the general will. In his article on "Political Economy" for Diderot's *Encyclopaedia*, after saying that the first rule for the men who govern a community is to conform to the general will, he proceeded to address himself to the question which this raises:

"How may one know what the general will is in cases where it has not been made evident? Is it necessary to assemble the nation in each unforeseen contingency? There is the more reason not to assemble it because there would be no certainty, in cases involving particular issues, that its decision was the expression of the general will; because such an undertaking would be impracticable in the case of a large population; and because it would rarely be necessary when the government is well intentioned: for the leaders know well enough that the general will always supports the side most favorable to the public interest—that is, the most equitable side—so that it suffices only to be just in order to be sure of following the general will."

Rousseau assumed, here, an unquestionable idea of justice on which decision can be based. Remote as he was from the existential world, it was possible for him to reason as if the only issue of politics was the choice to be made between what was known to be right and what was known to be wrong. Under the circumstances the concept of a general will becomes secondary, since the choice of the right must be the right choice in any case. What he was saying in effect was that in the perfect world of ideas which his mind inhabited men always will what is right.

What Rousseau meant by the general will was something quite different from that occasional predominance of voices with which we identified it in the last section. From the beginning, all thinkers who have taken the long view have meant something different from such a predominance by it. Thus Mr. Walter Lippmann points out a fundamental distinction between "the people" as those who constitute the voters on any particular occasion and "the people" as a continuing community which embraces the ancestral generations and those yet unborn. The living voters, at any particular moment and on any particular issue, are quite capable of betraying the permanent views and interests of the community for which they pretend to speak.

If, on every issue that arises, there is a clear right and a clear wrong, then the duty of those who govern is simple. It is to impose the right. Even the argument for popular sovereignty, which might otherwise embrace the right of the people to be wrong, supports such imposition where what is right represents the general will *ipso facto*. In effect, then, Rousseau's thesis authorizes any faction which believes itself to have infallible knowledge of the right to impose itself on the community by whatever means are required, and to do so in the name of the community.

The public, Rousseau had said, "must be taught to know what it is that it wills." At the age of twenty-five Karl Marx wrote: "We develop before the world new principles out of the principles of the world itself. . . . We simply show it for what it is actually struggling, and consciousness is something that it must acquire, even though it does not wish to." Here is an early expression of the thesis that the Communist Party knows infallibly what "the people" wills even when "the people," because its "consciousness" is insufficiently devel-

44

oped, does not know. In dualistic terms, one could say that the Communist Party is the sole bearer of the one idea that represents the veritable human propriety, unknown until Marx discovered it. The propriety is not less proper to people just because they do not yet recognize it.

This logic has its bearing on such events as occurred in Budapest in the fall of 1956, when military force was used to impose "the will of the people" on that overwhelming majority of the inhabitants who were "enemies of the people."

The Communist Party of the Soviet Union, as the repository and chosen instrument of Marxist-Leninist truth, alone knows what the people wills. But the Party, as a corporate person, is itself an abstraction from the world of ideas. During the 1950's a struggle went on among its leaders to determine who should formulate its infallible position on what the people wills. The tendency was for the authority of the Party to be concentrated increasingly in one man. The culmination of such a tendency is at the point where one man alone knows infallibly what the people wills. Just as those who dissent from the views expressed by the Party constitute "enemies of the people," so those who dissent from the views of the triumphant man in an intra-Party conflict constitute an "anti-Party group."

Up to this point we have assumed that the concept of "the people" embraces the total population, at least of the living. The references to "enemies of the people," however, now tells us that this may not be so.

SECTION 12

What the revolution of modern times did was to transfer the power and authority of the state from a sovereign who had a physical embodiment to one who did not. It transferred sovereignty to an idea called "the people." However, since political sovereignty has to be exercised in the existential world by physical persons, this raised the question of how to know what the will of "the people" was, or of how to know who was qualified to say what it was.

From the beginning, two separate answers were made, one identified with the Jacobin tradition carried on today by the Communists, the other with the liberal tradition represented by the Western democracies. Robespierre had no doubt that the Jacobin Society, which he dominated, was qualified to express "the will of the people" and was therefore entitled to have the power of the state delivered into its hands. The English and Americans preferred the procedure of counting noses to find a consensus and then simplifying the result by eliminating minority opinions from the final picture.

The liberal procedure has had the effect of assigning a greater value to the views of some persons (those who vote with the majority) than to the views of others (those who vote with a minority). But even those who vote with a minority are still considered members of the community called "the people," with all the rights of membership—for "the people," basically, is the entire population. "This is," said President Theodore Roosevelt, ". . . a government of the people; including alike the people of great wealth and of moderate wealth, the people who employ others, the people who are employed, the wage-worker, the lawyer, the mechanic, the banker, the farmer; including them all, protecting each and every one. . . ."

By contrast, the Jacobin tradition, basing itself on the concept of class struggle, equates "the people" with a part of the total population only. It is a social class conceived of as a corporate person. To Robespierre, aristocrats were not included in the concept of "the people." They were, rather, "enemies of the people," to be fed to the guillotine.

To the Communists, likewise, capitalists and bourgeois intellectuals are "enemies of the people." In Communist societies "the people" may actually be a small minority of the total population, as was the case in Russia in 1917 and in Budapest in 1956.

The two worlds, the world of ideas and the existential world, can never be completely without correspondence, if only because the latter is drawn to model itself on the former. The idea of "the people," therefore, has its copies in flesh-and-blood.

If all the individuals in a community had identical thoughts and desires, if all willed alike, this would not make the community a single person with a single will, for the corporate person is simply a metaphor. It would, however, provide a perfect basis (a basis without exception) for a generalization that corresponded to the idea of one people with one will. Perhaps something approaching this perfection has been attained by the bees. It is far from attainment by men. Nevertheless, in particular circumstances and to a degree however limited, the idea has had its recognizable semblance in flesh-and-blood.

The Jacobin concept, that society consists of two classes of which one is "the people," had more plausibility in France in 1789 (and Russia in 1917) than it would retain once the revolution had been completed. For centuries the population of France had been recognizably divided into a small aristocracy, which ruled in its own interest, and multitudes whose rather different interests were on the whole disregarded by the ruling aristocracy. The aristocrats could be readily distinguished from the multitudes by their clothes, their speech, their manners, their education, and their attitudes—all representing ideas of propriety applicable by severe reservation (as in the case of sumptuary laws) only to themselves. Other ideas of propriety applied to the rest of the population. Under these circumstances "the people" were like the inhabitants of the besieged city, possessing an exceptional degree of solidarity promoted by the oppression

47

they endured in common. The aristocrats were in the position of the besiegers.

Before the French Revolution the power to rule had been vested in the king, who was identified with the aristocracy. Under his authority, his power was shared with his fellow aristocrats. Therefore it could be said that the power to rule was vested in the aristocracy. The purpose of the Revolution was to take that power away from the aristocracy and give it to "the people," to transfer it from the one class to the other.

No one in the circumstances of 1789 would have found that these corporate concepts confronted him with a major intellectual dilemma. Any political philosopher might have found a ready answer for the question how an abstract concept called "the people" could actually exercise the power to rule. Assuming the solidarity of the respective classes and the identification with them of their individual members, he might have observed that the aristocracy, which was also an abstraction, could be said to rule because the power was exercised by an aristocrat. If the two species of which the state consisted were cats and dogs, and if a cat ruled it, then the substitution of a dog as ruler might well be considered the transference of power from the cats to the dogs.

Even in the circumstances of the eighteenth century, however, this view is too simple; the gap is too wide between the idea and the existential reality. Robespierre—a litterateur, a lawyer, and a dandy—could have had little in common with a peasant from the Vendée, for instance, or a Marseilles dock-hand.

Once those who had been identified as "the people" were no longer associated together by suffering at the hands of a common oppressor, the differences among them would become increasingly evident. Even though the state were ruled by a peasant, he would be an unrepresentative peasant; and his son, brought up in the palace, would be no peasant at all. Although a Robespierre or a Lenin, at the moment when he

48

seizes power, may have a background of experience or sentiment, at least, that causes him genuinely to identify himself with "the people," the experience of power is bound to corrupt him in his representative character. It is bound to corrupt him by teaching him things that his former comrades can never know, as well as by confronting him with the intractable and unexpected requirements associated with the maintenance of his power. Achieving greatness, he will illustrate Lord Acton's dictum that great men are almost always bad men.

So the tension between the idea and the existential reality increases. The supposed correspondence between them becomes in time a matter of oratorical cant only. Still, however, the Jacobin ruler justifies his rule, in a formal or rhetorical sense, by the claim that he represents an entity called "the people." Still he speaks in its name. Still, as it fades, he tries to keep it in existence by appealing to nationalistic or class feeling, by insisting on the continuance of the menace which "the enemies of the people" once represented. But his government is based on an increasingly evident fiction or, if one prefers, a fraud—as all government in this dual world of ours must, in some degree, be based on a fiction or a fraud.

SECTION 13

Both the liberal and Jacobin procedures are based on the premise that, among the forms of being in the existential world, there is a personal entity called "the people." Orthodox Marxists conceive of this entity as singular, a worldwide social class which will at last (when its enemies have been eliminated) comprehend the entire population of mankind. Nationalists conceive of it as plural, as represented by many "peoples" or "nations." In either case, the existential reality fails in large measure to conform. It remains excessively imperfect in terms of the perfect idea.

49

The problem posed for the political theorists is that of individuals or groups who dissent. Jacobin tradition solves it by limiting the concept of "the people," by excluding and outlawing the dissenters. It refuses to accept as legitimate the diversity of human opinions and attitudes in the existential world. Whoever establishes "the people," Rousseau tells us, must be prepared to change human nature so as to eliminate individual diversity. He must be prepared "to transform each individual, who by himself is a perfect and solitary whole, into part of a greater whole from which he receives in some fashion his life and his being; to alter the constitution of man in order to reinforce it; to substitute a partial and moral existence for the physical and independent existence that we have all received from nature. He must, in a word, take away from man his proper faculties in order to give him faculties that are foreign to him and that he cannot use without the help of others." The modern psychological techniques called "brain-washing" respond to this need.

Jacobinism is universalistic and authoritarian. It takes an *a priori* logic as its point of departure and insists on the conformity of existential circumstances. Liberalism, on the other hand, is more nominalistic and empirical. It tends to take existential circumstances as the point of departure and to adjust its logic to them. Where Jacobinism begins with a general will, defined in advance, to which individual wills must submit, liberalism begins with individual wills and tries to find a general will in them. Where Jacobinism safeguards the concept of "the people" in its purity by excluding those who do not conform, liberalism disregards the nonconformists when it comes to announcing what "the will of the people" is, but does not cast them out. They retain their rights of membership. So liberalism compromises the purity of the concept in order to provide for the rights of dissenting individuals and minorities.

50

The liberals are always seeking a middle way between the idea and the existential reality; and, as always happens when men seek a middle way, they do not walk single-file along a narrow path but they spread out, rather, over a broad belt of middle ground, some tending to one side, some to the other.

The tension between liberalism of the left and liberalism of the right has existed since the beginning of the democratic revolution. The liberalism of the right has been marked by that alarm at prospects of majority tyranny which characterized Edmund Burke in England, Alexander Hamilton and George Washington in America, making them hostile to the French Revolution. The liberalism of the left was represented most soberly by Thomas Jefferson, who was willing to take some risks of injustice to minorities for the sake of majority rule. And from the first there have been extreme liberals of the left whose thinking has had a strong Jacobin cast, who have been unwilling to compromise the concept of "the people," who have been alert to expose any "enemies of the people." There is a point, then, at which the liberal and Jacobin traditions merge. We must think in terms of a spectrum rather than of categories.

The concept of one people with one will, to the extent that it is vivid in men's minds, has far-reaching consequences, not only for the autonomy of the individual, but also, as we shall now see, for the conduct of international relations.

CHAPTER IV

THE LOCUS OF RESPONSIBILITY

SECTION 14

Moral responsibility belongs to persons, whether individual or corporate persons. If we maintain with Paley that only individual persons really exist, then we must hold that a nation cannot be responsible for good or evil, even for the good or evil done in its name, that it cannot be subject to reward or punishment. On the other hand, to the extent that we think of nations as corporate persons which really exist as such, it will seem right that they should be held accountable, that they should be punished for misdeeds attributable to them. The question that this raises bears directly on the great issues of war and peace in every age.

In every age the concept of communities as morally responsible persons, subject to reward or punishment, has tended to prevail. In every age, however, it has also been questioned by dissenting individuals. An early example occurs in the eighteenth chapter of Genesis.

Three wayfarers come to where Abraham is sitting by the door of his tent at the noonday hour of rest. One is Yahweh, on a trip of inspection, the other two are angels accompanying him. Abraham invites them to the midday meal. After the meal the three set out to continue on their way to Sodom, about which Yahweh has heard some disturbing reports which he means to investigate. Abraham goes with them to set them on their way. At this point Yahweh tells Abraham what the purpose of his trip is. "Because the outcry against Sodom and Gomor'rah is great," he says, "and their sin is very grave, I will go down to see whether they have done altogether according to the outcry which has come to me; and if not, I will know." The passage continues:

52

"So the men turned from there, and went toward Sodom; but Abraham still stood before the Lord. Then Abraham drew near, and said, 'Wilt thou indeed destroy the righteous with the wicked? Suppose there are fifty righteous within the city; wilt thou then destroy the place and not spare it for the fifty righteous who are in it? Far be it from thee to do such a thing, to slay the righteous with the wicked, so that the righteous fare as the wicked! Far be that from thee! Shall not the Judge of all the earth do right?' And the Lord said, 'If I find at Sodom fifty righteous in the city, I will spare the whole place for their sake.' Abraham answered, 'Behold, I have taken upon myself to speak to the Lord, I who am but dust and ashes. Suppose five of the fifty righteous are lacking? Wilt thou destroy the whole city for lack of five?' And he said, 'I will not destroy it if I find forty-five there.' Again he spoke to him and said, 'Suppose forty are found there.' He answered, 'For the sake of forty I will not do it.' Then he said, 'Oh let not the Lord be angry, and I will speak. Suppose thirty are found there.' He answered, 'I will not do it, if I find thirty there.' He said, 'Behold, I have taken upon myself to speak to the Lord. Suppose twenty are found there.' He answered, 'For the sake of twenty I will not destroy it.' Then he said, 'Oh let not the Lord be angry, and I will speak again, but this once. Suppose ten are found there.' He answered, 'For the sake of ten I will not destroy it.' And the Lord went his way, when he had finished speaking to Abraham; and Abraham returned to his place."

Apparently the Lord did not find even ten righteous in the city of Sodom, for he "rained on Sodom and Gomor'rah brimstone and fire from the Lord out of heaven; and he overthrew those cities, and all the valley, and all the inhabitants of the cities, and what grew on the ground."

One must conclude from this that even infants at their mothers' breasts, who could not themselves have committed sinful acts, were adjudged to have a share in the general guilt and so were included in the general destruction.

If we take account of the fact that the Yahweh of the Pentateuch is shown to have human limitations, we may suppose that he did not grasp all the implications of Abraham's questioning. For the moment he fell into a logical trap: he accepted the tacit premise on which the questions were based, that the city of Sodom was plural rather than singular. But as soon as he was once more on the road he must have reverted unconsciously to his original assumption that it was a single person, a corporate entity capable of sinning as such.

The misunderstanding between Yahweh and Abraham has manifested itself in all times. It is, however, particularly relevant to the period that begins with the revolution of modern times, when the doctrine of popular sovereignty (hence, popular responsibility) became the premise of politics.

SECTION 15

As the First World War approached its end, as preparations got under way for a treaty of peace, the essential issue that had divided Yahweh and Abraham arose to divide the victorious allies. This was the issue of "war guilt."

From the moment when the United States entered the war against Germany, President Woodrow Wilson tried to limit the identification of the enemy and the attribution of guilt to certain elements in the German community rather than to the community as a whole. Addressing Congress on April 2, 1917, he said:

"We have no quarrel with the German people. We have no feeling toward them but one of sympathy and friendship. It was not upon their impulse that their Government acted in entering the war. It was not with their previous knowledge or approval. It was a war determined upon as wars used to be determined in the old unhappy days when peoples

54

were nowhere consulted by their rulers, and wars were provoked and waged in the interest of dynasties or of little groups of ambitious men who were accustomed to use their fellow men as pawns and tools. It will be all the easier for us to conduct ourselves as belligerents in a high spirit of right and fairness because we act without animus, not with enmity, toward a people or with the desire to bring any injury or disadvantage upon them, but only in armed opposition to an irresponsible Government which has thrown aside all considerations of humanity and of right and is running amuck. We are, let me say again, the sincere friends of the German people and shall desire nothing so much as the early reestablishment of intimate relations of mutual advantage between us. . . ."

In repeated statements, Wilson made it clear that peace could not be made with the Kaiser and his government, that if they remained on the scene the allies "must demand, not peace negotiations, but surrender." He also made it clear that, once they left the scene, peace with the German people would be automatic—for they were not the enemy, the guilt was not theirs.

But his view was not the view of the preponderance of men and women in the allied countries, who had identified the enemy in their hearts, not as certain individuals among others, but as a single and sovereign people animated by a general will. It was this view that prevailed. When the Kaiser and his associates were at last gone from the scene, when they had been replaced by what Wilson called "veritable representatives of the German people," it transpired that the victors were not prepared to accept his distinction between the guilty and the righteous.

No peace was made with the accredited representatives of the German people in 1919—if the definition of a peace is a genuine agreement to restore amicable relations on a basis of equality. They were excluded from the peace conference, kept waiting outside the closed doors until the victors had prepared the document which they were required to sign. Article 231 of that document read: "the Allied and Associated Governments affirm and Germany accepts the responsibility of Germany and her allies for causing all loss and damage. . . ," etc. No mention of the imperial government which Wilson had said was the only responsible party. The Weimar Republic, required to expiate the war-guilt, was not to be admitted to the international society of the postwar world. It was brought low and held low in a posture of humbleness.

So it remained until it was at last able to recover its feet by its own devices.

SECTION 16

At Paris in 1814 and 1815 the same issue arose among the peace-makers as was to arise, again at Paris, among the peace-makers of a century later.

The increasing separation between the idea and the existential reality, after the French Revolution, is exemplified by the rise of Napoleon. At no stage does he look altogether like a representative of "the people," and he has come to look quite unlike one by the time he has himself crowned Emperor of France in the setting of a new French court. But he does not cast aside the theory of the Revolution, and the exploits of his armies have begun, at least, with the revolutionary justification that they are liberating "the people" of neighboring countries from the rule of the aristocracy.

Moreover these are not professional armies, like those of the past. They are popular democratic armies, displaying for the first time the spectacle of "the nation in arms." The common people of France, now feeling that the state belongs to them, that the state is the nation, feel for it that new ardor of nationalism which makes them willing to fight and die for its cause, as they would not have been when the state belonged to Louis XIV.

Few of us would doubt today that Napoleonic France was guilty of misbehavior on the international scene. But where, specifically, was the locus of guilt? Was the long course of aggression that upset the life of the civilized world and exhausted Europe attributable to Napoleon as an individual or to the French people, for whom he was acting?

The victors who drew up the peace-settlement after the defeat of Napoleon had the question at the backs of their minds. But the world they had been brought up in, the world they now undertook to restore, was essentially the pre-revolutionary world in which "the people" were politically inert and, therefore, without responsibility. The idea of popular sovereignty was not vivid for them. What they ended by doing, therefore, was to remove Napoleon and to restore the Bourbon dynasty by setting Louis XVIII on the throne. That done, there was no longer any enemy on the scene and peace was, in effect, automatic. France, under the restored Bourbon monarchy, soon took her full and honorable place again in the "family of nations."

No one, at the time, doubted that the preponderance of the French people had enthusiastically supported Napoleon in his aggressions. It follows that retribution and restitution might have been exacted of them as it was to be exacted of the German people a century later, and on the same basis of justification. What was essentially different in the two cases was not the existential reality but the ideas that invested and shaped the minds of the respective victors. Peace was made in the one case and not in the other because, in the one case, the peace-makers were acting in accordance with the ideas of Bossuet, in the other they were acting in accordance with the ideas of Rousseau.

SECTION 17

The issue that divided Yahweh and Abraham did not quite come to the surface in 1815 because all the victors, as children of prerevolutionary times, ended after some hesitation by attributing the actions of the state to the will of one individual. It did not arise in 1945, at the end of the Second World War, because all the victors, as children of post-revolutionary times, attributed the actions of the state to the will of the people (in the case of the Western allies) or (in the case of the Soviet Union) to that of the enemies of the people. It could be made in 1919 only because the régime that was identified with the origin of the war, basing itself on pre-revolutionary theory, recognized no obligation to represent a general will. This provided a basis on which a student of constitutional forms, like Wilson, could escape the implications of popular sovereignty.

In the Second World War the Western allies conducted their military operations and planned the post-war settlements on the premise that the world was divided between "peace-loving" and "aggressor" peoples. Their spokesmen were explicit in stating on repeated occasions that the governing régimes in Germany, Italy, and Japan were acting as agents of the respective peoples, that the evil which they represented was in the people themselves. Under the circumstances, the elimination of these régimes would not eliminate the evil. "It is clear to us," President Roosevelt told the Congress, "that if Germany and Italy and Japan—or any one of them—remain armed at the end of this war or are permitted to re-arm, they will again, and inevitably, embark upon an ambitious career of world conquest."

This being so, it would not be possible to conclude a peace with them when at last they had been overcome. Wilson, attributing the war-guilt to the Kaiser's régime, had said that, if it remained on the scene at the end of the war, the

58

allies "must demand, not peace negotiations, but surrender." Roosevelt, attributing the war-guilt to the peoples, who necessarily would remain on the scene, rejected peace negotiations in advance and announced that nothing less than "unconditional surrender" would be accepted.

This view of corporate guilt, with its implications for a postwar settlement, was expressed in its absolute form by Morley Roberts in a book published in London in 1941 and called *The Behaviour of Nations*. The following passage from the introduction reflects the Jacobin propensity for adhering without compromise to the world of nominal ideas:

"I shall speak of the State, or national organism, as a living, breathing 'animal,' since breathing is what the word means, which belongs to a low-grade invertebrate order not yet recognized by classical zoologists, although it is possible that a few biologists in their private meditations have ventured so far into the unknown.

"The question whether it is legitimate to call that an animal organism which is composed of the protoplasmic units called 'men' in various slightly different classes, castes, or tissues, surrounded by a semi-permeable protective frontier, or membrane: which increases, spreads into new territory, or buds and creates colonies, separate or attached to the parent; which can protect itself and even absorb or destroy like beings: which continually seeks nutrition to keep in work its inchoate tissues, organs, and machinery: which demonstrably exhibits as a whole in its low-grade plane all the physical and physiological phenomena of life: this question, I say, must be left to those, not already convinced, who have the patience to read this essay without prejudice. . . ."

The difference between Roberts and Rousseau is that, while the latter undertook to describe the existential world as it might be, should be, and on rare occasions was, the former pretended to be describing it simply as it was, like a natural

59

scientist reporting his observations upon a dissected frog. From his absolute premise he proceeded to draw absolute conclusions, rejecting any moral distinction between Adolf Hitler and the other "protoplasmic units" of the German body-politic. European chancelleries, he wrote, "know that the Germans' leader became their leader because he is so essentially what the Germans are." And again: ". . . we are being told that if Germany discards Hitler all will go well, that the Germans will cease to be Germans, and may safely be admitted as citizens. They are, however, cunning enough in defeat to discard him, while attributing to him tribal acts long meditated." This image of the German people as a corporate person with a general will secretly meditating evil, leads him to a logical conclusion. "If the Germans are again overcome," he writes, "it must be held that the massacre of a whole population is justifiable if no other means can secure an inoffensive nation or nationality."

President Roosevelt had recognized this same logic; but as a politician he lived in the existential world and he belonged, as well, to the liberal tradition that rejects the tyranny of any *a priori* logic. In announcing the objective of unconditional surrender he said: "This doesn't mean destruction of the people in those unhappy countries, but total and merciless destruction of the machinery *they* [emphasis supplied] have built up for imposing totalitarian doctrines on the world." When the end of the war was finally in sight he said again: "The German people are not going to be enslaved, because the United Nations do not traffic in human slavery. But it will be necessary for them to earn their way back into the fellowship of peace-loving and law-abiding nations."

All is summed up in a few words from the governing directive of April 1945 to the Commander-in-Chief of the United States Forces of Occupation in Germany. Under the heading, "Basic Objectives of Military Government in Ger-

60

many," they are: "*a.* It should be brought home to the Germans . . . that the Germans cannot escape responsibility for what they have brought upon themselves. *b.* Germany will not be occupied for the purpose of liberation but as a defeated enemy nation. . . ." The war is over, the Nazi regime has been destroyed, but the enemy remains and there can be no peace.

In 1815 the theory of the ruler's sole responsibility made peace automatic once the ruler had been removed from the scene. In 1945 the theory of "the people's" responsibility made peace impossible, even after the ruler had been removed from the scene.

As transpired in the event, it was not feasible to carry out in its full harshness the policy that had been formulated to govern the occupation of Germany. A principal reason for this, as we shall now see, arises out of the disparity between the two worlds in which we live.

SECTION 18

In time of war it is the abstraction that dominates the thinking of belligerents. But when the victorious forces at last march in to occupy the territory of the defeated enemy, the abstraction is suddenly subjected to a confrontation with the existential reality. A period of confusion ensues in which determined efforts are made, chiefly by those still at a distance, to uphold the abstraction as a basis of policy.

The words spoken by Roosevelt and the policy projected by Stalin during the Second World War leave no doubt that they had in mind a harsh treatment of the German nation after its power had at last been overcome. Moscow, moved by an *a priori* logic that allowed no compromise, actually subjugated the part of Germany that came into its hands; subjugated it at first directly and then by the imposition of a government that could speak for an *a priori* general will, whatever the will of individual Germans. But the Western powers also intended the subjugation of the German people; at least they intended their subjugation for an indefinite period of years until, in the President's words, they should "abandon the philosophy of aggression," until they should "earn their way back into the fellowship of peace-loving and law-abiding nations."

The sense of justice and self-protection alike entered into these plans. It seemed just that, regarded as a nation that had committed a crime, Germany should be punished; regarded as a demon nation, it seemed essential that it be kept in bonds. There was no conflict of motives here. But the image on which these conclusions were based was the wartime cartoonist's image of Germany as a ravening monster lashing a world of slaves. It was inevitable that when the Western troops entered Germany to establish their occupation the existential reality, now imminent and visible as it had not been before, would tend to replace the abstraction in their minds.

The conflict between the two was epitomized in the paradox of "fraternization with the enemy." The phrase itself reveals the two elements of the conflict in the two concepts that it opposes to each other, enmity and fraternity. The abstraction is one's enemy; the existential reality is one's fellow man. The high command, at a distance from the scene, tries to maintain the dominance of the abstraction, making fraternization a moral offense subject to discipline. But the occupation soldier is struck by the thought that these are regular people after all, and that the girls are very much like the girls back home. Invited to Sunday dinner in the home of a German family, he is touched by their human sympathy and generosity.

A Morley Roberts will cry out that the soldier should not be deceived, that under the sheep's clothing of the concrete lurks the wicked abstraction which represents reality. It may, in fact, be true that the particular Germans who welcome the American soldier to dinner were a year ago asserting the claim of the Teutonic race to be the master of mankind. But, having suffered defeat, this idea of propriety has been generally discredited. Remorse has entered their hearts, in all likelihood, and their kindness now is genuine. Not only are they under the sway of another idea of propriety now, the abstraction of "the enemy" has been replaced for them, too, by the concrete reality of an individual who is not essentially different from their own kind.

A few weeks after Americans had dropped atomic bombs from a lofty distance on two Japanese communities they were rushing medical help to the particular victims—men, women, and children—whom they discovered on the ground when they entered Japan; and it would have been a mistake for the Japanese to have doubted the sincerity of their compassion on the grounds that their policy of a few weeks earlier had showed them so resistant to the claims of compassion. This, too, was fraternization after enmity, based on the substitution of the existential reality in the minds of the victors for the abstraction on which the bombs had been dropped.

All this did not come to pass without that inner conflict which is the fate of a humanity that must live as best it can in two worlds at once. A few years after the Second World War it was common to see German tourists gazing at the bomb-craters around St. Paul's in London, and English tourists looking at the bomb-craters of Frankfurt, shaking their heads and blinking their eyes as if to free themselves from the cobwebs of an irresolvable perplexity.

63

CHAPTER V

THE VALIDITY OF IDEAS

SECTION 19

THE dilemma of mankind, we have noted, is like that of the visionary who cannot know whether a particular vision comes from God or Satan: if the semblance of the Archangel Michael, standing before him in a dream, orders him to go and slay his neighbor, he should wish to assure himself that it really had been Michael before obeying the order.

But how could he do so?

In any state of civilization, rudimentary as it may be, a man's will responds to nominal concepts, whether they are generalizations of existential realities or ideas of propriety. Because the consequences of acting on any particular concept may be terrible, he should wish to assure himself, first, of its validity.

But how?

A generalization of existential realities may have awful implications for action, as in the case of Morley Roberts's generalization of Germany, where the implication is genocide. An idea of propriety may have implications no less awful where it moves men to impose it on their neighbors, as in the wars of religion or the Communist movement today. Before acting upon the implications of concepts in either category, then, one would wish to test their validity.

What tests can we apply?

In the case of generalizations, which pretend to represent things as they are, the test is that of their correspondence to the things they pretend to represent.

64

The test to be applied to ideas of propriety appears to be less simple, since their validity depends, rather, on their correspondence to the *Logos*, of which we have knowledge only through the ideas that are to be tested against it. Is it not as if we were asked to test the validity of images in a mirror by what we saw only in the mirror's reflection?

In fact, however, there are two mirrors, for the *Logos* is reflected not only in our ideas but also in the existential world that imitates it. If these two mirrors are independent of each other, each separately reflecting the *Logos*, then each should provide a check on the other. Then the imperfect reflection in the one can be tested against the imperfect reflection in the other.

This raises the question whether the two mirrors are independent of each other.

It seems to me evident that they are independent although related, the human mind itself being an existential phenomenon. All of us may have latent in our minds a pattern of logic that reflects the *Logos*, but it is only the experience of existential phenomena in our environment that brings this pattern out—as the chemical developer, applied to the exposed film, brings out the photograph that is latent upon it. It is only in viewing the pencil-marks of this existential world that I am aware of the idea of the straight line which they imitate imperfectly. Praxiteles could not have conceived the idea of his Hermes, and executed it, if he had not familiarized himself first with the human form as it is found in the world of physical specimens.

Observation of imperfect physical specimens is what prompts, in the mind, ideas of their perfection. This is to say, then, that a test of our ideas of propriety is their relevance to the existential world. The perfection of the pencil-drawn circle is the perfection of circularity, not of straightness. The perfection of the human form is not the perfection of the insect form, with its six limbs instead of four. The hive,

65

though it represents the perfection of the bee's society, may be improper to human society; but we could hardly perceive that it was if we knew nothing of human society.

The reflection of the *Logos* provided by the existential world is not, in its essentials, of our making. Each of us is born into it and finds himself having to accept it as it is. We have to accept the fact that the human form has four limbs and the insect form six, that circles are circular, that stars are radiant, that water is wet. Our ideas of propriety, on the other hand, are subject to alteration by our own undertaking. If, then, there is an inadequate correspondence between our ideas and the existential world to which they nominally apply—between our idealizations and the objects idealized—it is our ideas that are subject to correction. The correspondence between the *Logos* and the existential world is that between perfection and its imperfect copy. To the extent that our own ideas of perfection do not have the same correspondence to the existential world they do not reflect the *Logos*.

Correspondence to the existential world, then, is not a test of our generalizations only, it is a test of our ideas of propriety as well. The knowledge of existential reality that we need to discipline the one is the knowledge that we need to discipline the other. Italian painters and sculptors of the fourteenth century were unable to produce anything to match the Hermes of Praxiteles because they lacked the necessary knowledge of the human body. As a consequence of the scientific study of anatomy in the following century, however, they were at last able to produce, in Verrochio's David and in Michelangelo's bound slaves, expressions of the ideal that were a match for the work of Praxiteles.

Relevance to the existential world is a test that can be applied best by those who have come to know that world best. Ideas, like works of art and literature, may be matters of taste about which disputation is vain, but even those who hold this to be the case are wont to accord their respect to what they recognize as educated taste.

SECTION 20

Our ideas of propriety ought to follow from our knowledge of the existential world, since they are concepts of its perfection. Our minds ought to retrace the order of creation, from the existential object back to the idea of which it is an imitation.

We are not born, however, with knowledge of the existential world, and such knowledge of it as we may be able to acquire in a lifetime must still remain partial in the extreme. (How much of the existential reality of six hundred million Chinese, for example, can I come to know in a lifetime?) Since we have to put something in place of the knowledge we lack, if only as a basis for deciding how to deal with our existential environment, we fill up this vacuum of our ignorance with nominal concepts, whether generalizations or ideas of propriety, and so it is they that tend to come first. On the slenderest experience of existential reality, or on second-hand report of it, we build a nominal world that is entire in itself.

We take naturally to nominal concepts, while knowledge of the existential world comes only with cultivation. Born as we are in ignorance of that world, the pristine emptiness of our minds is quickly filled up with simple generalizations in lieu of such knowledge. The child believes, perhaps, that all Chinamen wear pigtails, that all American Indians grunt and say "how," that all Englishmen are aristocrats, that all Africans are cannibals.

While such concepts as these present themselves to us as generalizations, they may in fact represent ideas of propriety, the two being generally confused in our minds, as we saw in Section 6. If I say that Chinese children have black hair I am making a generalization that corresponds as nearly as need be to the existential reality. On the other hand, if I say that Chinese children under the old régime showed an invariable courtesy toward their parents, my statement, although still cast in the form of a generalization, refers to a Confucian idea of propriety which Chinese children succeeded in realizing only partially. It represents an "idealized" view, a confusion of the idea with the existential reality. This would be the case even more clearly if I said that the Christian population of the world was characterized by meekness and charity.

Karl Marx saw human history as simply the history of class struggle, in which economic considerations determine what people do, in which a certain dialectical logic determines the evolution of society, and in which all moves toward the inevitable end of one classless, stateless society from which human conflict has disappeared. This is an idea of propriety, of nature's plan, of the *Logos*. Succumbing to its appeal as such, we are moved to conform to it, to imitate it, to enact it in our own conduct. But Marx did not present it as such. Being a materialist, he scorned the concept of an idea that had its own independent reality. He claimed, rather, that his conception was a generalization at which he had arrived by the scientific observation of existential phenomena.

To test Marx's concept as a generalization, we must ask to what extent it conforms to the existential reality as it is. To test it as an idea of propriety we must ask to what extent it represents the perfection by the standard of which the existential reality is imperfect (as the circle, rather than the straight line, represents the perfection by the standard of which the dented circle is imperfect). In either case, we must consult the existential reality.

The addiction to nominal concepts in place of knowledge is most notable in the child. However, since we can never

68

acquire more than a little knowledge of the existential world, no matter how long we live, that knowledge must still be eked out with nominal concepts. All we can hope for, within the limits of a lifetime, is to acquire such a modicum of knowledge as will serve to test those concepts and, by showing the degree of their inadequacy or irrelevance, make us aware of our ignorance.

Our inevitable ignorance confronts us with dire personal problems that we cannot meet except by substituting these abstractions for knowledge. Otherwise, how could we save ourselves from a paralyzing perplexity that might threaten our sanity? Since the hundreds of millions of Chinese individuals represent a variety beyond the grasp of our minds, we put the one simple image in place of them all. The abstractions of Marxist philosophy likewise enable us to have definite views on virtually every question, and to act with assurance on virtually every issue. They give us an illusion of knowledge that saves us from a burdensome perplexity, perhaps from mental breakdown.

This dependence on the abstractions to which we have given our allegiance makes us instinctively resist any knowledge of existential realities that tends to discredit them. Consequently the mere opportunity for experiencing those realities is not enough. The mind must be disciplined to recognize them, however unwillingly, if their reality is to prevail against the preconceptions. If I begin with the concept that all Latin Americans are sensitive and poetical, and if my mind is undisciplined, any course of direct observation on which I embark will merely confirm that concept, whatever the reality. When I travel in Latin America I shall note with a thrill of recognition those individuals who illustrate it (who are "typical" Latin Americans) while instinctively refusing to recognize those who, having no correspondence to it, provide me with no basis of recognition.

However, although we are bound to resist the knowledge

69

of existential facts that constitutes a threat to our preconceptions, in an environment of thought and discussion such knowledge may hardly be excluded indefinitely. As long as our intellectual development has not yet been arrested, a process of slow accommodation takes place. We find little adjustments that we can make in our concepts to accommodate the facts. Without abruptly abandoning those concepts, we modify them imperceptibly, developing them so that they will not continue to correspond quite so uncomfortably with the facts that, in the course of our growing experience, intrude themselves upon us. By this slow process our concepts may at last be quite transformed.

This is part of the process by which we approach maturity, each in our degree. As it goes on we are able to bring an increasingly sophisticated judgment to bear on the validity of generalizations and ideas alike.

SECTION 21

We noted in Section 19 that it was only the experience of existential phenomena which brought out in our minds the pattern of order that reflects the *Logos*. Such experience, however, is not enough by itself; for by itself, as any of us may observe, it brings the pattern out more vividly in some minds, less vividly in others. There must also be sensitivity to the pattern, an aptitude for apprehending it in nature, and this varies from one mind to another. A surgeon, although he had a more complete experience of human anatomy than Verrochio, might still be incapable of the vision that Verrochio expressed in his David.

What, more precisely, is this pattern of order that we take to reflect the *Logos*, that is native to our minds, and that may be brought out by experience of the existential world?

It is what enables us to conceive of order at all, as distinct from chaos. It is what enables and impels us to arrange the particles of experience in associations that make them meaningful. It is what we call reason. It is what we call harmony when we make a distinction between a logical arrangement of musical tones and a chaotic arrangement. It is a pattern of logical relationships. It is, in a word, logic.

Logic manifests itself in the widest variety of forms. It manifests itself in any sentence that has a subject and predicate; in any mathematical formula; in our preference for musical intervals of an octave over those of a seventh. It manifests itself in the Second Law of Thermodynamics, in the Constitution of the United States, in Michelangelo's painting of life passing from the finger of God into the recumbent body of Adam.

This logic, the property in some degree of every human mind, is in its degree proper to the minds of the other animals as well. A bird manifests it when it takes shelter before a storm; a mouse when a passing shadow sends it into its hole; a fish when it darts at a fly on the surface above it. We assume that it exists outside us, but we recognize it outside only because it corresponds to what we have inside and are born with.

None of us, however, is equally sensitive to all the manifestations of this logic. Philosophers may be lacking in the appreciation of music, and not all musicians have an aptitude for philosophy. A mathematician may see nothing in Michelangelo's painting, and the painter may be unmoved by mathematics. Some persons appear to be born with especially keen faculties of perception, either in general or in terms of particular aspects of this logic. Others appear to be born with relatively dull faculties. To the extent that mind exists at all, however, there is an innate pattern of order by the expression of which its existence is made known—by which, in fact, it is defined.

Given the faculties of perception, their cultivation is necessary. We men must be taught to see. This, in fact, is the purpose of literature, art, and music: to make the pattern of the *Logos*, which is implicit in nature, more nearly explicit. The statue in the American Museum of Natural History referred to in Section 6 is an attempt to represent existential reality as it is. This is the way the anthropologist, and perhaps the surgeon, has been taught to see the female form. But the Aphrodite of Melos teaches us to see something more in it: that implicit perfection which is a manifestation of the *Logos*. As we become cultivated in the appreciation of the arts, then, or in the processes of reasoning, our knowledge of existential realities is deepened by insight, by a sensitivity to the real ideas that these realities imitate. By this cultivation of our minds—not only in the arts, but in religion, in philosophy, in the logic of languages, and in the sciences as well—we become better qualified to judge the validity of ideas.

The validity of ideas is tested, then, not only by knowledge of the existential world but by the cultivated faculties of the mind as well. Knowledge and cultivation of the mind are, alike, products of education, and their achievement is in its degree the criterion of maturity. The validity of ideas, therefore, is best tested by the judgment of the most mature among us.

Considering the limitations in knowledge and cultivation of even the most mature among us, this is not as reliable a test as one would wish, but it is the best we have.

SECTION 22

The concept of the *Logos* implies an absolute scale of values based on degree of correspondence to it. This scale is no less absolute because, seeing the *Logos* only as in a mirror dimly, we lack absolute knowledge of it. We know it only in intimations, but those intimations are more cogent as we grow both in knowledge of the existential world and in that discipline of the mind which enhances insight and so extends vision.

The fact that we lack direct knowledge of the *Logos*, upon which absolute values depend, invites denials that there are absolute values. Such denials, however, involve a paradox that we have already met: in denying perfection by pointing to imperfection we affirm the standard of perfection by which imperfection exists.

This is exemplified in James Joyce's *Ulysses*, ostensibly a work of denial in the nihilistic tradition of its day. What it ostensibly denies is the heroic vision of man represented by Homer's Ulysses. Homer showed his hero as godlike. In doing so, Joyce tells us, he was false to life as it really is. To show what life really is, Joyce replaces Homer's Ulysses with the ungodlike Mr. Leopold Bloom, whose adventures, because they are unheroic, correspond to daily experience as those of Homer's Ulysses do not. The apparent effect is to discredit the heroic vision by revealing the sordid imperfection which characterizes our world of physical existence as it actually is.

The real effect, however, is the opposite. Just as the existential reality of the Danish court is sordid only by the standard of Shakespeare's vision (which is Hamlet's), so the existential reality of Mr. Bloom's Dublin is sordid only by the standard of Joyce's vision (which is that of Stephen Dedalus). In a contrast of light and dark it does not matter on which of the two the artist concentrates: each must be equally intensified by the intensification of the other. Revolting against the idealism to which he has been brought up, Joyce emphasizes the sordidness by which that idealism is made only more poignant. His vision is affirmed, then, in its denial.

Perhaps he would have replied that the vision is an illusion, that only the sordid existential phenomena are real.

Here, in this thesis, the issue is drawn between the dual philosophy and those opposed philosophies—nihilism, positivism, materialism, nominalism—that deny the reality of anything except what is physically manifest. The nihilist says

73

that the idea of the straight line is an illusion, that only the marks in the visible world are real. In practice, however, he belies himself repeatedly. Looking at the mark left by the pencil, he complains at its lack of straightness, thereby judging it according to an idea of propriety the validity of which he rejects. He is in the position of the solipsist who, while he makes an unassailable case for the nonexistence of anything outside himself, cannot live according to it, but belies it in the very act of making it.

Surely it is proper to say of a particular idea of propriety, like Homer's, that it is an illusion; or even to say that all our ideas are illusory in some degree. We have already seen that an idea is valid only to the extent that it represents the perfection of its existential subject as it is, rather than as it is not. By this test, then, ideas, while not illusions as such, may be more illusory or less.

Joyce and his contemporaries represent, in part, a reaction against the Victorian Age, which had been dominated by an idea of moral respectability that was inadequately relevant to human beings as they are in existential reality. Recoiling from the false idea, from the illusion, they were disposed to find reality only in the solid physical phenomena of direct experience. Such phenomena are at least directly testable, while our ideas are all illusions in their degrees, to be mistrusted as such.

But those who deny that there is any world of reality beside that of physical existence continue to live in both worlds. All they can do is to pretend that they live in the one world only.

SECTION 23

The *Logos* is what gives direction and purpose to human history. Our mission is, knowing it first, to realize it in the world of existential reality. If ever the day comes when that

74

mission has been fulfilled, then we shall no longer live in two worlds, but only in one, and our dilemmas will be over.

Meanwhile we are still on the way. We still live concurrently in the world of actuality and the world of ultimate things. The ultimate things are apprehended by insights which can rarely be distinguished with certainty from meretricious conceptions or pretences or from the naïve conceptions of the primitive mind. There is, however, such a thing as educated judgment, the judgment in which all those who are the most mature, in terms of cultivation, tend to agree.

Johann Sebastian Bach, oppressed by the sordidness of the existential world, finds his escape in the composition of the B-minor Mass, which represents a world of perfect order and harmony. Another man, similarly oppressed, gets drunk and howls in the night. The judgment of the mature has no difficulty in comparing the two as higher and lower; the music of the Mass is closer to the *Logos* than the howling of the drunkard.

Confucius, Socrates, and Jesus would probably agree that Augustus Caesar represents a higher type of statesmanship than Caligula, that Abraham Lincoln represents a higher type than Adolf Hitler.

A critic might hold that the test, here, is simply a practical one, based on the difference between those who construct and those who destroy, those who build an order for the well-being of men and those who spread disorder to their detriment. But the practical test is not irrelevant: it refers to harmony and order, which we associate with the *Logos*. Men who are only practical operators, who are only technicians of organization and administration, are incapable even of great practical results. For the roots of harmony and order, from which the practical results arise, go deeper than mere pragmatism.

Both Augustus and Lincoln were moved by visions of the ideal world, but their visions were disciplined by knowledge

75

of the imperfect world. It is in his resolution of the tension between the two that an Augustus or a Lincoln is great. By contrast, a Caligula represents no coherent vision but simply an existentialist chaos; a Hitler represents a vision indeed, but it is the quixotic vision of a child, undisciplined by knowledge of the existential world. Like a child he substitutes false abstractions (e.g., of Jews and Aryans) for concrete realities. Such a vision can lead only to disaster when any powerful attempt is made to realize it.

The growth in maturity of the individual is growth in knowledge of the *Logos*. The same development takes place in societies, distinguishing those that are culturally advanced from those that are backward. Finally, this development takes place in mankind as a whole.

What we have to examine now is how it takes place.

CHAPTER VI

PROGRESSIVE REVELATION

SECTION 24

THE dual philosophy appears throughout human history in a variety of forms. All the world's religions represent it. Half of its formal philosophies are merely particular expressions of it. It is the assumption on which all creative activity in art, in science, or in politics is based. It is, therefore, the foundation on which civilization is built and on which, alone, it can be maintained.

Because it has this universality and permanence, we do better to think of it, not as a particular and transient philosophical system, but as philosophy itself. It would follow that the formal systems which stand opposed to it (positivism, materialism, etc.) are to be classified as anti-philosophy.

This philosophy is generally offered to us in the form of a simple mythology, and it is in this form that we are asked to believe it. To the people of ancient Greece it was offered in the form of those myths that told how the gods on Olympus first created a godlike "golden race" of men, how they replaced it with a less godlike "silver race," which they replaced with a grosser "bronze race," itself to be replaced, at last, by that pitifully defective race to which we of the present age belong. For the earliest Jews it took the form of the account in Genesis of the Creation and the Fall of Man. The doctrine of Original Sin is a related expression of it. In mediaeval legend the *Logos* is represented by the Holy Grail, the attainment of which depends on the attainment of human perfection. Lancelot, succumbing to the lure of the existential world, represented by Guinevere in the role of Eve, fails in the quest, which is achieved at last by his son Galahad, who is proof against all worldly temptation. In the legend of

77

Faust, the abandonment of the quest for the *Logos* in favor of existential satisfactions is the road to perdition.

Such myths provide a form in which a philosophy that is itself sophisticated can be communicated to those who are not. As successive generations grow in knowledge, however, losing their pristine simplicity, the essential absurdity of the myths, taken literally, threatens the continuance of belief. A Socrates, in such circumstances, is capable of directly grasping the philosophy itself, without its mythological trappings. Others, the half-sophisticated, fall into general unbelief.

Because the myths are so intimately bound up with traditional society, which is always obsolescent, they become the targets of those who are in rebellion against it. A Karl Marx denounces them (as "the opium of the people") in the context of a campaign that, going beyond mere mythology, becomes anti-philosophical. Philosophy, along with its mythological trappings, becomes the object of the nihilistic animus, since the radical destruction of society calls for the destruction of its philosophical foundations.

When the trappings fall into disrepute, the philosophy is liable to fall into disrepute with them. Then civilization suffers until again, now in some new guise, the renewed acceptance of the philosophy provides the creative motive and the discipline on which civilization depends.

The development of civilization represents the acquisition and translation of knowledge—knowledge of what is transient and, through it, knowledge of what is ultimate. The process moves unevenly. Sometimes its advance is rapid; again there is stagnation or retrogression.

When I was a very young man I adhered with a certain passion to the belief that human history is marked by the rise and fall of civilizations, each moving through an established and predestined life-history like any individual organism, from birth through growth, maturity, and decay, to death. I still think that this represents a discernible pattern and a plausible logic in human history as it has transpired so far. Like the Hegelian dialectic, it is not the sum and substance of all truth, now and forever, but an element of truth that enhances understanding, that explains what would otherwise appear to be without sense.

I can see this pattern plausibly applied to our own times. The increasing domination of our thinking, especially over the past century, by the various forms of anti-philosophy, together with the consequent decline of the arts, resembles the cultural evolution that marked the transition from the glory that was Greece to the increasingly sordid grandeur that was Rome.

But I have in mind and I dimly see the lineaments of a longer and larger progress, and it is to this vision that I now turn.

SECTION 25

At the end of Section 6 we saw that our minds inhabit a nominal world of ideas and of things which we suppose to represent the real world of ideas and things. Because the nominal ideas and the nominal things exist for us as names in the first instance, the logic implicit in their names tends to replace, in our minds, the logic implicit in their reality.

The crudest examples may serve. Taking two common species of wild plant, we name one "Solomon's Seal," the other "False Solomon's Seal," thereby establishing, in the nominal world of our minds, a relationship that is not matched in the world of reality (where the one does not pretend to be the other). Again, the English distinction between "to like" and "to love" does not exist as neatly in the nominal world of a Frenchman, whose language has, in place of the two English terms, only the term *"aimer."* Consequently, where a man brought up in French might find a friendship ripening into a grand passion, brought up in English he would fall in love or not fall in love. There would have to be an instant at which the emotion he felt stopped being that of the one nominal category and became that of the other. (This is exemplified by the spectacle of English-speaking boys and girls trying to decide whether they are or are not in love. The French language hardly allows the problem to arise).

Our nominal world, which is a world of our own imagining, differs from the real world in being composed of categories that are fixed. We had occasion to note this in defining a generalization; for a generalization belongs to the nominal world, being in the first instance a logical device for describing existential realities. While what "the green field" represents has no categorical character, since it merges into woodland on one side and desert on the other, the nominal term that we put in its place does have a categorical character.

Names, being categorical, remain unchanged while the realities for which they stand undergo a continuous transformation that may leave them, at last, quite different from what they had been when they were first named. Today the white European nation to which the name "Turkey" is applied bears no resemblance, in its existential reality, to the Mongoloid nation called "Turkey" that established itself at the eastern end of the Mediterranean ten centuries ago. But the unchanging name, standing in place of the changing reality, disguises this.

"Turkey" is a generalization of existential realities that we have categorized and fixed, for our imaginations, by the imposition of the name. We also categorize and fix ideas of propriety, for our imaginations, by the imposition of names—although the ideas themselves, as objects of men's allegiance, undergo a constant change that may at last transform them to the point where they are the opposite of what they had been.

In the nineteenth century Karl Marx gave expression to a

complex of ideas which he denominated "Communism." This "Communism" inspired an allegiance in his followers, who pledged themselves to its realization in the existential world. But the correspondence between the ideas set forth by Marx and the existential world as it actually was, inadequate to begin with, became conspicuously inadequate as the existential world itself evolved. The ideas, therefore, had to be adapted: they, too, had to evolve. When, at last, those who had dedicated themselves to the cause of realizing "Communism" achieved power over the Russian state, they found the existential circumstances with which they were at grips quite different from what had been assumed in the formation of the ideas. The circumstances being intractable, where a choice was posed between them and the ideas, they were necessarily governing. The ideas, then, had to be abandoned and replaced, or they had to be revised.

In the half-century that followed, the ideas that went under the name "Communism" were transformed or replaced to the point where they were not only different from the original ideas but counter to them in important respects. If Marx had returned to earth he might well have regarded what was still called "Communism" as representing a rival set of ideas, opposed to what he had stood for himself. But he would have found the name unaltered by one iota, and he would have found that this gave what it represented an aspect of immutability which made it seem an established standard around which the people of successive generations might rally.

In a world without known shape or stability, we men look for something to cling to as the swimmer looks for a rock. What most of us attach ourselves to in the end is a nominal symbol, a name, supposing it to represent the otherwise unknown object of our search. We attach ourselves to the immutable name, thereby escaping from the flux in which we might otherwise drown.

This explains the fact that men will line up for or against a name of which they cannot tell the meaning.

Nominalism, in disguising the process by which ideas are adapted to existential circumstances as they are, disguises the process by which mankind makes progress in the knowledge both of the existential world and, through it, of the *Logos*.

SECTION 26

What is Christianity?

Charles Darwin and Mrs. Darwin differed. "I can indeed hardly see how anyone ought to wish Christianity to be true," he wrote in his autobiography, "for if so the plain language of the text seems to show that the men who do not believe, and this would include my Father, Brother and almost all my best friends, will be everlastingly punished. And this is a damnable doctrine."

Annotating this passage after her husband's death, Mrs. Darwin wrote: "I should dislike [it] to be published. It seems to me raw. Nothing can be said too severe upon the doctrine of everlasting punishment for disbelief—but few now wd. call that 'Christianity' (tho' the words are there)."

Religions undergo a continuous evolution which is disguised by the retention of their nominal identity.

In the Pentateuch mankind, after the dispersal from Babel, was divided into nations among which absolute estrangement and total hostility were the rule. Each regarded the others as distinct species, not to be included within the circle of fellow feeling. If the others suffered, one could not appreciate the fact because one did not attribute the feelings of one's own kind to them.

The first books of the Old Testament present a picture of the world as it was seen by a society which was primitive to the point of savagery. If the thinking of these ancient people

82

is represented by Yahweh's thinking, then it is clear that they generally substituted the crude concepts of the corporate person and of multiple species, without qualification, for the existential reality of individuals. This they carried so far that the destruction of Sodom, the death of all the first-born among the Egyptians, or the extermination of the inhabitants of Jericho seemed an act of justice to them. They never knew that these alien people were individual human beings like themselves. They did not have knowledge of the concrete reality for which they substituted, like children in any age, dehumanized abstractions.

The religion of the Pentateuch, however, broadens out and becomes more civilized, more humane, gentler, and steadily more sophisticated. By the time one has reached the Book of Ruth the growing illumination is already apparent. In Ruth's story we have an anticipation of the parable of the good Samaritan, suggesting that those who are not our immediate kin may yet be our kind.

The New Testament, in passage after passage, is radiant with the illumination that we saw only in flashes against the decreasing darkness of the Old Testament. It represents the dawn of cosmopolitanism as opposed to the bitter nationalism of the Pentateuch, a broadening knowledge of the world of concrete particulars that begins to be able to accommodate universalism, the concept of a single mankind.

For the world of individuals implies universalism. When one begins to judge each man on his merits, nationality becomes irrelevant, and eventually the category that will hold best, in nominalistic thinking, is mankind. In the New Testament, time and again when the matter comes to a test, a man's faith proves more important than his nationality; perdition or salvation is by individuals rather than communities. The role of hatred is diminished by the creative role of compassion, which is an expression of fellow feeling.

But a candid reading of the Gospels, which does not overlook the passages that make a modern reader uncomfortable, suggests that the religion of the New Testament is still incompletely evolved. In it, hatred and compassion dwell side by side, a narrow nationalism persists alongside a humane universalism, there is still collective punishment for guilt attributed to the collective body.

The New Testament represents an advance over the Old. But it is an advance that has itself come to seem increasingly incomplete, until in the nineteenth century Mrs. Darwin and her neighbors, good Christians as they conceived themselves to be, could no longer accept some of its fundamentals ("tho' the words are there").

Today we may take a broader view of religious truth than was possible when men fought over the literal standing of the doctrine of transubstantiation. We can see that religious doctrine is an imperfect imitation of the higher truth that we men are able to glimpse only occasionally, partially, in uncertain flashes, and that the formalities of religion have the purpose of invoking such revelation. All religions, then, may represent the same truth, each in its own fashion, so that the validity of one does not obviate an equal validity in the others.

The hope of man's future is that the revelation which they represent will increase.

SECTION 27

Those who hold knowledge of the truth to be the product of divine revelation have sometimes suggested that revelation is progressive. Over the centuries it has been enlarged and refined. Perhaps it has kept up with an increasing human capacity.

For myself, I cannot think of the media of revelation as being confined to the literature called sacred. Considering the role of all literature as the representation of the *Logos*, it is all sacred. I would regard Shakespeare's *Hamlet* as a vehicle of revelation not essentially distinguishable from the Gospel according to John. I would regard Plato's *Apology*, the Book of Ruth, the *Sermon on the Mount*, and Lincoln's *Second Inaugural Address* as essentially equal vehicles of revelation. Going beyond what is strictly literature, I would regard the Aphrodite of Melos and the Cathedral of Notre Dame in Paris as essentially equal vehicles of revelation. I am not willing to say that some of these are revelations of God or the *Logos* while others are not. I cannot see any except a superficial distinction between sacred and profane music, between sacred and profane art.

In categorical thinking we may suppose that by the beginning of the Christian era the religion of the Old Testament had become inadequate. The increasing currency of Greek philosophy itself showed the growing sophistication of Mediterranean societies which made that religion increasingly inadequate. It was therefore supplemented or revised by the religion of the New Testament, which grafted the Greek tradition onto the Judaic.

Today, we might argue, the religion of the New Testament has itself become inadequate, not because it is less sophisticated than it was but because we are more sophisticated than our forebears. Under the circumstances, perhaps the world is moving toward some new religious advance. Perhaps it is ready for a "second coming" rather different from the first, at a still higher level of conception than the first, although perhaps no more than one more step closer to finality than the first.

But this possibility alone seems to me too crude for an uncategorical reality that does not progress by nominal steps. Lumping the sacred with what we commonly distinguish from it in literature, music, and art, I should think that progressive revelation has been proceeding all along, and not only by the categorical steps which we associate with the

85

birth of new religions. It has been proceeding in the works of Shakespeare, in Melville's *Moby Dick*, in Joyce's *Ulysses*, in Spengler's *Decline of the West*. It has been proceeding in the cantatas of Bach and the quartets of Beethoven, in Darwinism and in the theories of relativity associated with Einstein, in Gothic architecture, in nineteenth-century French painting. . . . I do not suppose that it proceeds evenly, either on the whole or in particular media of its expression. There was little of it in any medium in tenth-century Europe. Western music, surely, began to lose its inspiration by the beginning of the nineteenth century. And it may well be that the inspiration is failing everywhere among us today.

We must take the long view. If we go back to the world of the Pentateuch or the world of Homer, and if we follow the course of history to our present, we travel through periods of creative abundance and others of creative dearth, through periods of advance and periods of retrogression. But the impression is of an upward progress. One can hardly read even the works of Plato today without an awareness of how much more experience we now have of the matters with which they deal.

Every age represents a mixture of the primitive and the sophisticated. The predominantly primitive age of the Pentateuch is the setting for the sophistication of Abraham. The more sophisticated age in which we live is the setting for manifestations of savagery that correspond to manifestations of it in the Pentateuch. Hitler's abstraction of Jewry corresponds to Yahweh's abstraction of Sodom. Still, we are ahead of where we were three thousand years ago. The primitivism of a Hitler is more exceptional now than it would have been then, the sophistication of an Abraham was more exceptional then than it would be now.

This long-term, irregular progress may be less plausible to us today because of the blind alley in which our creative endeavor finds itself, limited as it is by the anti-philosophy

86

of our age. The premise that only what is material is real, because it reduces the purpose of such endeavor to the pursuit of illusions, deprives it of justification and incentive.

I do not suppose, however, that we shall remain forever blocked at this point, although we may be unable to resume our progress without the impetus of some new religious development such as that which inaugurated our Christian era.

The future is unknown to us. It may contain the extinction of our kind, which will join the dinosaurs in the graveyard of defeated hopes. Or perhaps we shall return to barbarism and a second chance. Or perhaps our population will fan out from the earth into space, with incalculable consequences. Perhaps we shall go on in greater or less confusion to some ultimate end—the scientific and technological beehive, or an apotheosis beyond our present conception.

Meanwhile, what matters is direction. Feeling the *Logos* within us as well as the animal, we must strive for its increasing realization. We must try to go on as best we can, in spite of obstacles of which the greatest is our ignorance, the darkness of our minds into which dim flashes of some reflected light occasionally penetrate. We must try to make things work. And in order to accomplish all this we must strive for an ever increasing knowledge of reality in both its aspects. It is in terms of this reality, and to this end, that we have to organize our society.

CHAPTER VII

THE ORGANIZATION OF MANKIND

SECTION 28

THE chapters that have brought us to this point have set forth a philosophy in terms of which we may understand the organized communities of mankind, those nominal entities that appear as the chief actors in human history.

Our organized communities belong to the nominal world. They are in the first instance ideas of propriety that we call nominal because they have their primary expression in nominal terms, in words or equivalent symbols such as flags and heraldic devices. So the United States of America, for example, is an idea that has its primary expression in a name, a declaration of principles, a Constitution, a body of laws, a flag, and so forth.

These nominal ideas are made manifest in the existential world by the behavior of individual men who act them out. The President of the United States is a physical individual filling a nominal role, acting out a nominal idea. This is equally true of all other physical individuals who identify themselves with the name "American," although their roles are lesser. The idea of the United States of America, initially taking the form of words and other symbols, moves them to think of themselves as members of an American community that has its own propriety; it moves them to conform to the principles, the laws, and the other nominal particulars of the idea; and it moves them to press such conformity upon their neighbors.

Any organized community, then, shows the universal duality of idea and existential manifestation. It is a nominal idea, perhaps perfect within its own terms, but imperfectly realized by the individuals who compose it. The consequent discrepancy is the source of contradiction and confusion. The observer of a particular community who was preoccupied with the idea and unmindful of the existential reality would have a different view of it from that of an observer who was mindful of the existential reality alone.

As we have seen, however, the idea in its simplicity has the greater appeal for our limited minds, which are bound to substitute abstractions for the existential variety and complexity that they cannot comprehend. Consequently it is only when the discrepancy between the one and the other becomes extreme—as when the existential reality comes to stand, for the most part, in direct opposition to the idea—that we may become poignantly aware of it and be troubled.

These, then, are the terms in which we must attempt to understand the world of nation-states in which we live.

SECTION 29

In the nominal world to which it belongs, each community is a personal entity like any individual person. We give it a proper name and a personal character, speaking of it as of a sentient being, ascribing to it happiness and misery, desires, interests, and passions.

Under the circumstances, it is not strange that ideas which to our minds represent propriety for the individual person should represent propriety for the corporate person as well. If the individual person, in our thinking, is entitled to life, liberty, and the pursuit of happiness, so is the community which we think of as if it were an individual person. If all men are created equal, so are all sovereign states. If individuals have the right to determine their own destinies, so do communities. Liberty, sovereign equality, self-determination—these are all ideas of propriety that we attach to the corporate person by transference from corresponding entities in the world of existential reality.

As soon as we do this, however, we invite the confusion, the contradiction, and the dilemma that spring from the discrepancy of the two worlds. For the propriety of the community may, in its realization, conflict with the corresponding propriety of the individual, obviating the possibility of its realization.

The dignity of the individual and the inviolability of his essential personality is an idea of propriety that dates back to the antecedents of Christianity, an idea implicit in the doctrine that man was made in the image of his maker (of the *Logos*). The essential fact about man was that, however great the preponderance of evil in him, he also contained a spark of divinity that represented a possibility of eventual apotheosis. The purpose of human life on earth was to cherish this spark and to work for the realization of the promise implicit in it. Human life might be sordid in fact, but it was distinguished by the possibility of being godlike.

Augustine and the early church, living in an age of dissolution and spreading anarchy, could look forward to the realization of this possibility only after death. With the establishment of the new feudal order after the Dark Ages, however, with the revival of Aristotelian thought, and with the renewal of hope for life on earth as men again began to build a civilization, it no longer seemed impossible that the promise inherent in man might be increasingly realized here below. In these new circumstances the ultimate purpose of social organization had to be that of providing optimum conditions for developing the potential if latent virtue which every man had within him.

In the Christian tradition, born at a time when the Roman Empire was disintegrating in a welter of sordidness, the state was essentially evil; and until the French Revolution there was little disposition to idealize it. This implied clearly that the authority of the state over the individual must be limited. Put the other way around, it implied human rights, the freedom of the individual. During the Enlightenment, and especially in the liberal democratic tradition that placed its emphasis on *laissez-faire*, the state was conceived to exist only as the guardian of liberty. The realization of the individual's unlimited possibilities, inherent in the possession of a soul or in the faculty of reason, depended on his being free, and the only purpose of the state was to protect his freedom.

"Freedom," then, came in time to join the ranks of those words which are invested with an aura of sanctity for successive generations of school-children. When it came to be applied to the corporate person it would preserve its sanctity even where it had lost its logical meaning.

Another such word is "equality."

Undoubtedly the roots of the concept that "all men are created equal" go back as far in Western history, or almost as far, as those of "freedom." In Christian thinking, every man's possession of an immortal soul made all men equal in what was essential, however unequal they might be in physical attributes, in aptitudes, or in social position. At least it put them beyond human judgments of inequality. When they came before the Judgment Seat on the day of the Last Judgment the king would have no advantage over the commoner: both would stand on the same level in the eyes of God. Then, as modern concepts of justice developed, it was accepted as a fundamental principle that all men were entitled equally to the benefits of the same justice, that all were equal under the law.

So "equality" joined "freedom" in the ranks of words, originally applicable only to the individual, which would retain their magic, if not always their logic, when applied to the corporate person of the state.

"Liberty" and "equality," in their latter-day application to communities, may be recognized under such designations as "independence," "freedom," "self-determination," "self-government," "nonintervention"—as well as under the original terms, often with adjectives like "sovereign" attached. Words like this tend to take on a life of their own and an intrinsic virtue, for us men, apart from any specific meaning. We will fight under the banner on which they are inscribed long after we have forgotten what it is they signify. On occasion we may even fight against what they signify.

SECTION 30

I once lived in a Latin American republic that had for its motto, inscribed on its official shield, the word *"libertad."* The country was governed by a general whose name one never mentioned without glancing around to see who might be listening. Citizens might be arrested by the police without charges against them and, before judicial proceedings could be instituted, might have met their deaths (according to the police) while trying to escape. Few families did not live in fear of the knock on the door in the early hours of the morning, the entrance of the plain-clothes police, and the abduction of the head of the household, whose disappearance forever would remain unexplained. In the prisons torture was systematically practiced, and it was not prudent to allow the evidence of it to survive. No words could be spoken in public, no printed matter circulated, without the approval of the authorities. No one might travel, even from one town to the next, without the permission of the police.

The word *"libertad,"* nevertheless, was not without a meaning on which every school-child was brought up. A century and a quarter earlier, the country had been part of a Spanish colony. When Spain had been conquered by Napoleon, the colony found itself independent. In the ensuing anarchy it had broken into five parts, each under the rule of a succession of local *caudillos,* and the republic I refer to, still under this kind of rule, was one of those five. The word *"libertad"* referred to the independence of foreign rule, the achievement of sovereignty, which marked the beginning of its national history.

An Indian proverb asserts that self-government (*swarājya*) is preferable to good government (*sūrājya*). I cite it here because it poses an alternative that, where it does present itself, has philosophical implications which go to the heart of our subject. We are to suppose a case in which a choice is to be made between a bad self-government and a good government under foreign rule.

The first question that arises is, what is meant by self-government. We have no reason to suppose that it means only government by the procedures of liberal democracy. The membership of the United Nations is confined to states recognized as self-governing. They include personal dictatorships, like that of the Latin American republic, and Jacobin states under one-party rule, like the Soviet Union. The definition by which all are accepted as self-governing is clearly a negative one. It is the absence of foreign rule. Any state that is not under foreign rule enjoys that self-government to which the Indian proverb refers.

What argument can be made, then, for preferring such self-government as that of the Latin American state to a government under foreign rule which, let us say, respects human dignity and assures individual freedom?

We shall find the answer if we read Rousseau, who above all others framed the nominal terms of the thinking that has since become the premise of politics the world over. To Rousseau the people constitute one moral person as a consequence of that initial social contract by which those who had formerly existed as individuals, in a state of nature, came

93

together and unanimously agreed to give up their individuality, merging themselves in one body politic. The specific terms of that contract, as Rousseau reports them, are: "Each one of us puts in common his person and all his powers under the supreme direction of the general will; and we receive each member into the common body as an indivisible part of the whole."

Rousseau's general will, to which all have surrendered their individual wills, is not literally a general will or an active consensus. It is, as we saw in Section 11, a euphemism for whatever is right by the test of the public interest, the interest of the corporate person created by the contract in place of the plural individuals who originally entered into it.

This is the premise of modern nationalism and of our contemporary international system. It is the premise of the Charter of the United Nations.

Viewed from outside, if not from inside as well, the nation-state is one moral person with a single will. No question can be raised, therefore, when the representative of the Latin American state signs, on its behalf, a document that opens with the words: "We the peoples of the United Nations...." In signing it he is expressing the general will of the people to whom he belongs.

Accepting the premise that each community is one moral person with one will, the question of self-government is the question whether that person is properly slave or free, whether he may properly be constrained to the will of another—a will which is committed to a self-interest not his own—or should, rather, be free to follow his own will, identified by definition with his own self-interest. The premise of the question excludes any consideration of the particles of which he is composed, which have no separate being, no separate will, no separate happiness.

Posed in these terms, the question of self-government versus good government virtually answers itself. Slavery,

94

even under a good master, is a violation of the propriety we call justice.

The argument for freedom joins at this point with the argument for equality. Each of the moral persons on the international scene equals every other as one equals one. Consequently it would be unjust, if one such person is free to follow his own will, to deny the same freedom to any other.

The transfer to the community of rights originally attributed to the individual raises no question except with respect to its premise; and the question of its premise has already arisen for us in the dialogue between Yahweh and Abraham which we had occasion to examine in Section 14. It may be useful to return to that question now, in terms of the philosophy which has since undergone a fuller development in our thinking.

SECTION 31

The Indian proverb supposes a choice between good government and self-government. More specifically, the choice may be that between freedom for the individual and freedom for the community. The question, in its essence, is which of two entities shall come first in our thinking. For Yahweh the corporate person had a reality that the individual person lacked; therefore it came first. For Abraham, the individual had the more vivid reality and came first.

What answer do we ourselves make?

Our answer, at last, must be that Abraham was right. The individual belongs to the world of existential realities, the community to the world of nominal ideas. The individual is real, the community not real. So we finish by associating ourselves with Paley's dictum: "Although we speak of communities as of sentient beings; although we ascribe to them happiness and misery, desires, interests, and passions; nothing really exists or feels but *individuals*."

The end of existential reality is to achieve, in its own self, the perfection of the *Logos*. Nominal ideas are means to this end, no more. At best, they are partial reflections of the *Logos*; at worst, impostures. They have no value in themselves, as nothing in the nominal world has any value in itself.

The perfection of our ideas of propriety to the point where they coincide with the reality of the *Logos* is merely a condition precedent to our end. Therefore to treat the organized community as the end for which we must be willing to sacrifice the individual is to commit an absurdity.

We stand on different ground when we cherish the community for the sake of the individual. Then, however we exalt it, we attribute no value to it in itself. We do not value its independence, self-determination, or sovereign equality in themselves. We value them only as conditions precedent (if that is the case) to the perfection of the individual. When the individual manifestly suffers from any of them, then we cannot justify it.

This is not a doctrine of individual self-sufficiency. Community is necessary for the individual's fulfillment, and the only question is what kind of community.

To this, then, we address ourselves next.

SECTION 32

We agree that community is necessary for the individual's self-fulfillment and that its justification is only in this. What we want to know, then, is what kind of community.

Those who, throughout history, have made the community absolute in their thinking have tended to exalt one community over all others. The corporate person, for them, cannot be divided into sub-persons or combined with others to make super-persons. In Yahweh's thinking, Sodom is indivisible and whole in itself. Rousseau warns that in the collective person of his vision there must be no other political associations among individuals, who have undertaken to give themselves unreservedly to the whole; and the world he envisages would consist entirely of such collective persons, each with an independent general will, each pursuing its own self-interest. The extreme nationalists of the nineteenth and twentieth centuries also represent this view.

However, the stricture does not apply to us, who are exalting no community as an end in itself. We do not, therefore, need to regard different kinds of community as mutually exclusive. We do not need to rule out the possibility that an individual might enjoy concurrent membership in a family, a city, a province, a nation-state; in Europe, in the West, and in mankind; giving allegiance to each in measure, to none without measure.

We begin with the individual, his human nature, and its needs. By himself he is a beast, like the child of countless legends who, separated from his parents at birth, is reared in the woods by wolves. Even if we suppose that in the course of his lifetime he learns something of existential reality and something of the *Logos*, he will not be more able than the beasts to communicate it to his casually begotten child, and each generation will start from where he did.

Human progress, as it has been manifested since the days of the cave-men, depends on the communication to each generation of the knowledge accumulated by its predecessors. This is possible to any extent only where the means of recording and communicating knowledge are organized.

In every generation the individual by himself is limited in the knowledge he can gain and store. If he wishes to avail himself of knowledge beyond these limits, he must be able to consult others who have made themselves knowledgeable in matters that he himself has not mastered. This also requires organization.

Again, if he wishes leisure to learn, he will depend on the

97

benefits of economic specialization, which also must be organized.

All this is to say merely that the progress of mankind has to be a cooperative undertaking. It depends on a community of endeavor among men.

Again, the individual has a poor chance of protecting himself against all the hostile elements in the natural environment, including hostile individuals, if he does not stand guard with others, sharing a common burden on the basis of a common interest.

Aside from such crude needs, he has psychological needs or a desire for psychological satisfactions that cannot be met alone. The positive satisfactions that exalt life in the family are matters of our common experience. By himself the individual can have no purpose or hope beyond survival, which cannot be long and will likely be short.

Other writers have labored these points, which need only be mentioned here. What we may best do here is to look at the whole matter of human community—the needs it has to fill, its possibilities, its limits—in exemplary terms.

SECTION 33

I write these words in a Swiss Alpine village, one of several included in a commune. The individual lives his life in the intimacy of this commune, which is his community in a sense that Switzerland, a more abstract and remote concept, cannot be. It is like his family. In fact, if he is typical a large proportion of the population is related to him by blood. If his roof is falling in and he, himself, is incapacitated, the commune will repair it for him. Perhaps he blows a trumpet in the local band and looks forward to the sociable evening rehearsals. He knows and is known by everyone.

This commune is in the Canton of Valais, which joined the Swiss Confederation in 1815 but, having been independent, is thought of as an autonomous member of an association. The Confederation, from its earliest history, has been an association of cantons for their mutual defense, and it still retains much of that character today, although with minds shaped by the prevailing political pattern of the world we have come to think of it as a nation-state. The local mountaineer, like every other Swiss, has his primary citizenship in his canton, and it is from this citizenship that, secondarily, he derives his Swiss citizenship. He refers to the men of other cantons, not as compatriots but as "confederates," and for one of them to take up residence in his canton he must, like any foreigner, obtain permission.

The Confederation (i.e., Switzerland), with its headquarters at Bern, has to do with my Valaisian chiefly in connection with the joint military defense for which it was created. The federal tax that he pays (much smaller than the cantonal) is denominated "Tax for the National Defense." In addition the federal authorities require him once a year to go off with fellow members of his Canton and with confederates for two weeks of military service.

Beyond the Confederation there is no organized political community for the Swiss. The Canton belongs to the Confederation, but the Confederation, in accordance with Swiss neutrality, belongs to nothing, not even the United Nations. The cosmopolitan Swiss whose horizons are wide may nevertheless be acutely aware of belonging to Europe, an ancient community now threatened, as so often before, from the east; and, beyond that, to something larger called "the West" or "Western Civilization."

Here, then, is an expanding series of communities with which the individual may identify himself, from his immediate family to Western Civilization. And I daresay that if the earth were attacked tomorrow by Martians he would quickly identify himself with all mankind. He stands at the center of a series of concentric circles.

Add to this that, as a Valaisian, our mountaineer also belongs to the Roman Catholic Church, which is an expanding series of communities in itself, from the parish to the oecumene.

What is to be noted about this individual is that none of the communities to which he belongs asserts a claim to monopolize his allegiance. This absence of an overriding claim by one community in the concentric series distinguishes the Swiss from the preponderance of men today and reveals, by its peculiarity, what is the essence of nationalism.

The communities that form a concentric series around the individual differ in kind as well as size.

A community, we have said, belongs to the world of nominal ideas, and it follows that the small family living in one household must also be a nominal idea. Any member of a family becomes conscious of it as such when he thinks of its family characteristics. For the most part, however, the existential reality of the members is more vivid than the idea, being a matter of intimate knowledge for which he has no need to substitute abstractions.

This is only less true of a local community like the Alpine village, or like the commune, where everyone knows everyone else.

The case of the canton is different. Because the citizen cannot even visualize the Canton of Valais as so many individual human beings he has to put a nominal concept in place of their reality. He knows only the idea, the individuals being beyond his ken. This idea is compounded of sensory impressions, of what was taught him about Valaisian history and geography in school, of confused memories of poetry, song, and oration, of heroic fables, of the symbol of the Valaisian flag. When he goes off on military service, where he associates with confederates, he is prepared to uphold the honor of the Valais against the slights which the sons of rival cantons may be prepared to cast upon it.

The family and in a lesser way the commune serve the individual's need for love, for being known and cherished. The commune, because it is greater, affords him a security that the family alone could not provide. The canton, on the other hand, does not satisfy his need for love and personal relations. What it satisfies is his need to identify himself with what is strong and imposing to other men. Feeling his own insignificance in this great world, he gains a vicarious security and a sense of power by associating himself with this majesty. The Valais, unlike the family or the commune, can give him this fulfillment because it is a legend, a nominal idea, not diminished as such by any vivid presence of the imperfect existential realities to which it refers. The abstraction holds a largely unchallenged sway.

Today, however, the Valais lacks one qualification for meeting this need. It lacks sovereignty, independence. It has become part of a larger whole, of a greater majesty to which it is constitutionally subordinate. The Valaisian, consequently, has (in principle) the choice of joining with others to achieve the independence of the Valais, its sovereign equality with every other independent state in the world, or of shifting his allegiance to Switzerland, which has the independence and sovereign equality that the Valais lacks. For evident reasons, the latter choice has the advantage and, generation by generation, the citizens of the cantons come increasingly to think of themselves as Swiss nationals, to identify themselves with the sublime protective goddess, "Helvetia," who perpetually stands guard with spear and shield in the image on their coins.

But isn't Switzerland, too, part of a larger whole? Does she not belong to Europe, or to the Atlantic community, or to the West, or to Western civilization?

Here, in our expanding series of concentric communities,

we again come to a change in kind. Up to this point the communities, which are associations by likeness, have had form and coherence given them by common organization—which, as we have seen, imparts a categorical definition that the community otherwise lacks.

Europe surely is as much a natural community as Switzerland. The French-speaking Swiss Catholic who has come to identify himself with the German-speaking Swiss Protestant ought to have no greater difficulty in identifying himself with his French-speaking Catholic neighbor in France. In terms of natural community, the Italian-speaking Swiss canton of Ticino, overlooking the Po Valley, belongs more to the neighboring communities in Italy than to the German-speaking community of Basel on the Rhine.

But Europe lacks the definiteness of outline which constitutional form (association by common organization) would give it. It is not a sovereign state with one political constitution, one government, one capital, one flag. Under the circumstances, the idea of Europe remains inchoate in the mind of the European, without outline or vivid personality, and so does not exercise the compelling attraction that the formally organized sovereign state exercises on his loyalty.

The same is true of "the West," of "the Atlantic community," or of "Western civilization."

Every man lives at the center of a widening complex of communities, of which the major ones tend to be concentric to one another. These concentric communities differ in kind as well as extent, from the extreme of the family to that of the civilization. They compete with one another for the allegiance of the men who inhabit them, and in this competition the nation-state has a peculiar advantage today, as the city-state yesterday, in the combination of formal organization and the attribute of sovereignty. Prevailing legend makes it seem that the artificial element of form contributed by statesmen and lawyers simply gives expression to realities already existing in nature. The individual, awed by what is so great and fulfilling, believes easily.

SECTION 34

In addition to the individual's need for love (which is met by the small community), he feels the need of identification with a might and majesty that he is conscious of wanting in himself.

This need may be variously met. It is commonly met in our day by identification with the idea of the sovereign state. In the prophetic vision of Rousseau, the individual sacrifices his dignity and independence as an individual only to partake of a greater dignity and independence. He enjoys a vicarious happiness in the happiness of the state, considering its attributes as his own. If the state is free he is free, no matter what servitude it imposes on him.

Here, then, is one idea of human propriety. We are asked to consider its validity, which is its correspondence to the *Logos*; and, while we do not know the *Logos* directly, there are tests we can apply. One is that of correspondence to existential reality as it actually is. The other is that of logic.

First, the test of logic.

Our mission as men is to realize in ourselves the perfection of the *Logos*. We have recognized that progress toward this realization cannot be made by the solitary individual, that a community of endeavor is required. Accordingly no achievement is altogether that of the individual alone. The cultivation that he represents is a cultivation that the community has imparted to him. Some of the greatness of Socrates was Athens.

The community, however, is a nominal concept, not an independent reality. Existing only in the minds of individuals, it is merely an emanation of them. As such, it cannot be greater than they are. Individuals may be inspired by the greatness of a concept, but it is individuals who have conceived it to begin with. If, then, some of the greatness of Socrates was Athens, the greatness of Athens was altogether that of Solon, Themistocles, Pericles, and the other Athenians.

To Rousseau, however, and to all collectivists since his time, the concept has had the primary reality. The individual has been a citizen, a member, a statistic, a particle, but nothing in his own right. In Rousseau's vision, in Hegel's, in Marx's, the community has all greatness in itself, its members having surrendered their individuality to it. It is itself a person, standing independently, with an independent personal will. Although perhaps none of its members would share this will as individuals, as constituent particles all share it on the basis of its rightness *a priori*, knowing that where they might differ they would be wrong. It is their will by abnegation of their own individual wills.

This vision is the product of a confusion, the confusion that we first saw manifested in Yahweh's conception of Sodom. When the nominal is substituted for the real, the real becomes secondary. So it becomes possible to degrade individuals and to inflict unspeakable suffering upon them for the sake of the concept that has been put in their place.

The fault of Rousseau and Marx was in this confusion of the nominal and the real. Nevertheless, we could justify what they did if we could accept the premise on which they did it.

If, as we hold, there is one perfect idea of man which all individuals imitate, which it is their mission to realize, then in the hour of its realization all individuals must become identical in their conformity to its perfection; the many must be reduced, again, to one; in place of a multitude of imperfect wills there must remain only one perfect will, which is the *Logos*, which is (if we may use traditional language) the will of God. In that hour the distinctions we now make will be obsolete: for then, at last, the nominal will coincide with the real, the existential will coincide with the idea that was its model.

The only error that absolutists like Rousseau and Marx make (but it is a fatal error) is to assume that mankind has at last come to the threshold of this finality, that it has reached the stage of being ready, now, to proceed to it.

Viewing existential reality as it still is (this being the other test), we shall not ourselves make that mistake. Our problem, still, is not to constitute the final perfect community of mankind, but to constitute the form of community best adapted for the progress toward that end of a notably ignorant and imperfect mankind.

SECTION 35

The discrepancy between the two worlds in which we still live is the source of our difficulties. For we have to make our plans in terms of the one and to carry them out in the other. This confronts us with unavoidable contradictions.

These contradictions are exemplified in the disparity between the nominal and the real everywhere. The United States was founded on the principle that all men are entitled to life, liberty, and the pursuit of happiness; yet slavery continued to be practiced in it for almost a century. It was founded on the principle that governments derive their just powers from the consent of the governed; yet for four years it found itself fighting to subjugate the Philippine people, whom it did not want under its jurisdiction.

The men who conduct governments know, if others do not, the force of circumstances which compel them at every turn to act in disregard of the principles by which they had intended to govern their actions. None could have had more reason to know this than the men who made the French

Revolution, intending to carry out the ideas of Rousseau, or the men who made the Russian Revolution, intending to carry out the ideas of Marx.

To deal effectively with this dual world, we must be conscious of its duality and the limitations it imposes on us, for we cannot succeed in riding the two horses if we think of ourselves as riding only one.

The fault of the Jacobin tradition is in the disposition to think only in terms of an *a priori* logic that pretends to be the *Logos* itself, the original model for the creation of the world. Such thinking requires either a tacit disregard of the limits set by existential circumstances as they are, or an overt refusal to accept them as they are. Rousseau in his *Social Contract* exemplifies both. In his chapter on the legislator he asserts that whoever would undertake his proposed transformation of human society would need the abilities not of a man but of a god. This implies that he is not thinking of the transformation as a program to be put into effect. For the moment, at least, what he is writing is a work of fiction like More's *Utopia*.

In the same chapter he also exemplifies the overt refusal to accept existential circumstances as they are; for the task which only a god could perform, but which is essential to the realization of the new society, is that of effecting the total transformation of human nature.

In 1789, twenty-seven years after the publication of the *Social Contract*, the outworn structure of society in France at last collapsed. In the consequent emergency some new structure had to be erected as quickly as possible to take its place. So men like Sieyés and Robespierre, who had been captivated by Rousseau's logic, found themselves undertaking the task which only a god could perform.

No one less than a god could abruptly change existential circumstances in their essential nature to conform to a logic that, being *a priori*, does not take them into account. In a million years, perhaps, they will change; but in any man's lifetime they will prevail, still, over the logic that demands their conformity. The blood which bathed the streets of Paris in 1793 was the evidence of their intractability.

Rousseau, tending always to reject existential reality, was happy only in the conceptual world. The opposite fault is also common, although those who commit it do not write books to exemplify it. They are the pragmatic men of action, preoccupied with immediate circumstances. In the world of ideas they are like those unsophisticated tourists from an alien environment who stand before the European cathedral not knowing what it is they are supposed to appreciate. They live in the nominal world because this is the destiny of mankind, but to meet its demands they can arm themselves with nothing better than the clichés and catch-words which they offer as their philosophy.

Where such men come to predominate, creativity is lost. In default of an adequate model, life fails of purpose. Sordidness invades the whole structure of society. It was such men who presided over the decline of the Roman Empire, which survived from generation to generation only as some ancient tree remains standing after it is dead.

We ride two horses and must try to keep one foot firmly on each. This we can do only if we manage so as to keep them from moving too far apart. But, to keep them from moving too far apart, we must master them both.

SECTION 36

If we men are to continue our progress we must have constantly in our minds a nominal model for our imitation. This model must have the greatest possible validity, which is to say that it must correspond to the *Logos* as closely as may be. In addition it must not be too far apart from the existential reality which we represent.

If we accept this we accept with it the dilemma of our world's duality, and the tension that must continue as long as the dilemma has not been finally resolved by death or the completion of our evolution. The dilemma and the tension are in the discrepancy between the *Logos* and existential reality, to both of which the nominal idea must have its relevance.

These are the terms within which we have to deal with the problems of human society.

We must also deal in terms of mankind as a whole.

Until our century it had seemed enough for political theorists to design models of the local community almost as if it would find itself alone in the world. Neither Plato nor Aristotle concerned himself with the problem of organization on a scale larger than the city-state, and twenty-two centuries later it was still possible for Rousseau to do his thinking essentially within the same bounds.

Today, however, the world has become too narrow and crowded for such limitation. When the masses of our kind are virtually continuous over the land surfaces of our planet, when all of us live from the fruits of all its lands, and when it can be encircled in an hour by one of our engines, then mankind is the smallest community that is self-contained and self-sufficient.

This implies the reform of an ancient defect in our nominal thinking. The limitation of community, hitherto, to the scale of tribe or nation has been accompanied by a conception of mankind as divided into opposed species. The children of Yahweh have been distinguished from the children of Baal, aristocrats have been distinguished from commoners, "peace-loving nations" have been distinguished from "aggressor-nations," as though the distinctions were genetic, like that between cats and dogs. The concept of the two species ("we" and "they," the good and the wicked) has dominated the history of mankind to our own present.

The logical implication of the concept is, as we have already seen, genocide. If the world is divided between the good and the wicked, then the triumph of the good implies the destruction of the wicked. "The only good Indian," said the North American pioneer, "is a dead Indian." So Yahweh destroyed the people of Sodom; so the children of Yahweh, when they captured Jericho, destroyed the children of Baal; so the representatives of the people of France put the aristocrats to the guillotine; so the Nazi regime in Germany undertook the extermination of the Jews; so we Americans were able, in 1945, to destroy the people of Hiroshima and Nagasaki.

The fact that the concept of the two species (in its various forms) implies genocide should not cause us to dismiss it if it meets our tests for the validity of nominal concepts. If we have reason to believe that it does faithfully represent the existential reality for which it stands, then the extermination of the wicked may be an obligation of the virtuous.

In fact, however, it typifies the thinking of the immature more than that of those who have ripened in the knowledge of existential reality and the discipline of logic. The contrast between Abraham Lincoln's attitude toward the defeated people of the South and that of most of his fellow citizens in the victorious North, a contrast between sophistication and simplicity, is repeated time and again throughout history, beginning with the eighteenth chapter of Genesis.

Similarities are not as susceptible of definition as differences because they lend themselves less readily to the process of analysis. The method of science, in a strict sense, is analytical, a procedure of taking things apart. For putting things together, for establishing valid associations, one depends rather on the intuitions of the creative imagination, of the generalizing eye, as expressed chiefly in the arts or the humanities (although expressed under the rubric of science by a Newton or an Einstein). This requires a greater sophistication.

"Not long ago," Clifton Fadiman wrote, "I happened to observe a mother lifting her eight-year-old boy in her arms. As she did so she laughed and said, 'You're getting so big you'll be lifting me soon.' It was the simplest of statements. Yet I felt something transiently touching about the scene merely because millions upon millions of mothers reaching back into the dawn of history must have said the same thing to their children at some time and because other millions will say it in the remote future long after this mother and child are dead."

It is this recognition of oneself in others, this discovery of experience common to all men, that contributes the moving element in humanistic art. This, we say, is universal experience. What the American mother said in the twentieth century a Jewish mother said in the days of Joshua, and if the language was different the difference was superficial only. And the Egyptian mother who was to lose her first-born before the prediction of his growth could come true; the Chinese mother in the mud compound on the banks of the Yellow River, in the time of Confucius or two thousand years later—it is all the same; the Japanese mother in the corner of her garden under the cherry blossoms, in the evening of too warm a day as at last the sun sinks upon the horizon; the Viking mother on the banks of the fjord, whose man has gone south in the long-boat for the raiding season, and who says to the little boy that he will have to be her man now until his father comes back (wondering, as countless women have, whether he ever will); the African mother, naked at the river's edge, placing her son astride her hip; the Roman matron or the English lady or the Macedonian peasant woman; the American Indian mother outside the tepee on the Great Plains, or my wife—all know the thought, the attitude, the emotion, the essential experience.

It is the same with Pieter Breughel's painting of a frolic at the village tavern, the children playing games, slipping between their elders' feet, getting into mischief, and half their elders merely bigger children than they—five hundred years ago as it might be today, in the low countries as it might be here. Or Vermeer's painting of the cook, the brawn of her arm pouring the milk from the pitcher as the afternoon sun comes through the kitchen window to make the scene golden—just like the peasant girl in our kitchen now, stopping to shoo away the children who want to know, eternally, when it will be ready. The scene repeats itself for thousands of years (the golden light of the sun on evenings then as now), while the individuals who enact it are replaced generation after generation, different and forever the same. Vermeer's peasant girl is taking her turn in an eternal pageant.

Or Abraham dozing at his tent door "in the heat of the day," until the unexpected approach of such honored visitors brings him to his feet, half ashamed and confused at having been found napping—and then the stir indoors where Sarah, the eternal housewife, never yet surprised, must perform the eternal feat of hospitality with briskness and laughter. (One can see old Sarah's arm pouring out the milk, like the cook's in the painting by Vermeer, like that of my wife or the girl in the kitchen now.) Or Sarah, learning that she and Abraham are to have a child of their union when they are already beyond the age for such things ("After I have grown old, and my husband is old, shall I have pleasure?"), saying: "God has made laughter for me; everyone who hears will laugh over me." This is not Jewish life in a legendary past but the life of mankind forever.

The record of history and the arts is full of such testimony. One finds it in Thoreau, or a Chinese artist of the Sung

Dynasty, looking at a kingfisher. One sees it in the idealist Augustine (or Marcus Aurelius), made hopeless by the politics of his day and seeking escape in philosophy; in Hamlet's revulsion against the nastiness of the Danish court; in Thucydides, appalled by the folly and destruction of war twenty-five centuries ago, offering his account of "the past as an aid to the interpretation of the future, which in the course of human things must resemble if it does not reflect it."

The concept of opposed species does not do justice to the basic humanity that these similarities represent. The dehumanization of the foreigner, the image of one's antagonist as a demonic being, the implicit denial that human pleasures and human sufferings, human strengths and human weaknesses, human virtues and human vices, are to him as to us— this is based on an inadequate appreciation of existential reality.

We have seen how, since the days of the Pentateuch, the progress of human knowledge has been increasingly inimical to a narrow parochialism, how in the most mature minds (those that represent the frontier of progressive revelation) it has found its expression in a concept of man's universal brotherhood. With the disappearance, at last in our time, of the physical circumstances that separated our communities in the past, the ancient concept that denies the common humanity of all must appear increasingly obsolete.

SECTION 37

The more vivid the individual person, in our thinking, the less vivid the corporate person. For when we look at the corporate person we see the variety within, and we see the similarity without (by extension of the variety within), until at last there are no frontiers short of those that embrace the whole of mankind.

It is between these two poles, the individual and mankind

rather than the individual and the nation, that we have to devise a workable reconciliation.

Our purpose in such a reconciliation is to make progress toward perfection. Is the perfection toward which we would make progress that of the individual or that of mankind? The question implies a contradiction that does not exist, for the perfection of the one must be the perfection of the other. When men are perfect, their association, too, will be perfect.

In metaphysical terms it is possible to contemplate a progressive conjoining and ultimate merger of all the particles of being—of atoms to form molecules, of molecules to form organisms, of organisms to form compound bodies, and so on—until at last, in the long course of evolution, all being has become one. This carries us, however, beyond the bounds of practical philosophy, which can have its application only in the world as it is known to our experience. From that world Paley's individual has not disappeared, nor can his disappearance be foreseen.

We do not know what the nature of a perfect association among perfect men would be; but at least until the instant of its final achievement the difference between the nominal and the real would persist, and Paley's dictum would still hold good. Accordingly we must still regard the perfection of the nominal as no more than a means to the perfection of the real. The association of individuals must still be for the sake of individuals.

Addressing ourselves, then, to the world as it is, we acknowledge our present ignorance of what it should be. We reject the absolutism of those ideologists who assume that they stand at the end of man's intellectual evolution, knowing at last what constitutes his true propriety.

The implication of our ignorance is the acceptance of diversity. If there is progress to be made in the knowledge and imitation of the *Logos*, then the effective imposition on mankind of one idea of propriety, to the exclusion of all others, would stop it; for that progress depends on a process resembling natural selection, requiring a variety of alternatives. Men must be free to reject ideas that have been found wanting in the light of experience or logic. They must be free to develop them or replace them with others freely offered.

We must therefore wish to see such organization of all mankind as insures freedom of thought and expression, providing safeguards against the impositions of any absolutism. One way to insure this is to prevent any of the communities that advance rival claims on the allegiance of the individual from achieving a monopoly of that allegiance; for any community that makes itself absolute in this respect must tend to impose, on the minds of the individuals whose whole allegiance it has gained, the absolutism of an intellectual orthodoxy. It follows that the kind of political world we should work for is one in which the frontiers of various communities criss-cross one another, in which a stabilizing tension prevails among them all, in which each is checked by the others to prevent it from becoming absolute.

This means that we must resist the absolutist claims of the nation-state. In such a nation-state as I described in Section 30, for instance, we should be glad to see a strong church in a relationship of some rivalry with it; we should welcome vested interests of workmen, of businessmen, or of other groups that also provided a check on it, while themselves being checked by it and by one another; and we should welcome the impact of ideas of propriety from without, representing wider communities that compete with the state for the allegiance of its inhabitants.

What I am describing is a multiple balance of power, world-wide and ubiquitous, in which none of the associations involved can gain an unlimited ascendency. I would have such a system prevail within the nation-state, over the larger world to which it belonged, and in terms of other frontiers crossing its own—until its own frontiers came to be less formidable than in our day, until a single system of checks and balances could be discerned over the whole area of mankind.

Such an organization of mankind would not work well, however, where men were not governed by a respect for limits. They would have to accept as normal and salutary the existence of diversity, of rival systems of thought and rival views, of competition in the market-place under a regime of freedom that set limits to what the competitors might do to one another.

So we get back to the knowledge of our own ignorance, which is basic. For men will not set limits where, out of ignorance, they believe that their views are God's views, or that they know infallibly what "nature" or "history" intends for mankind. We men can practice toleration of diversity only when we think of ourselves as searchers, all searching alike for a truth of which we have intimations, but that none of us has yet found. Then any issue must be merely that of opinion against opinion. But where we conceive an issue to be that of truth against error we cannot practice toleration; for the righteous may not tolerate the wicked, the spokesmen of God may not tolerate the servants of Satan.

Socrates alone among his contemporaries was wise enough to know his own ignorance. Only the growth of a like wisdom among us can make freedom secure. Only by its virtue can we maintain the conditions necessary for progress in the knowledge and imitation of the *Logos*.

SECTION 38

We live in the dim nominal reflection of two worlds, a primary world of perfect ideas and a secondary world of imperfect imitations. Our common mission is to realize in ourselves the perfection of the primary world. This is what gives purpose and direction to our lives.

The common mission requires common endeavor, and common endeavor requires the organization of our society. What gives purpose and direction to our society, then, is what gives purpose and direction to our individual lives. By it we may test the alternative possibilities for the organization of that society.

But all must fail if we fail to recognize both worlds and the nature of our involvement in each. If we try to conduct our lives and organize our society on the basis of an anti-philosophy, refusing to look beyond the imperfect world, then the long progress that has already taken us so far from our primitive condition will lapse. Then, without purpose or direction, we shall fall into confusion, perhaps producing in some final catastrophe the failure of the promise we still hold.

So law and organization are important, but at the bottom of all is philosophy.

✧

For our knowledge is imperfect and our prophecy is imperfect; but when the perfect comes, the imperfect will pass away. When I was a child, I spoke like a child, I thought like a child, I reasoned like a child; when I became a man, I gave up childish ways. For now we see in a mirror dimly, but then face to face. Now I know in part; then I shall understand fully, even as I have been fully understood.

—St. Paul, *I Corinthians 13*

PART TWO: AMPLIFICATIONS

Note: All references in Part Two to passages elsewhere, in either Part One or Part Two, give the number of the Part in letters, then the Section number in Arabic numerals, and then (if the reference is to Part Two) the particular passage in italic numerals, thus: "See Two, 27, *3*."

PART TWO

AMPLIFICATIONS

SECTION I

"[The concept of two worlds] has been basic to philosophy and religion from primitive times." The earliest known example of the concept of two worlds is in the "Memphite Drama," written by Egyptian priests around 3500 B.C. Professor Tomlin writes that "all the great thinkers of mankind have observed a distinction between spiritual and material reality, and that they have attempted to explain the latter by reference to the former and not the other way round."[1]

SECTION 2

1. *"There must have been an idea of man before there were men."* By itself the statement is too simple. Man is in process of an evolution that might transform him, at last, into what we would not call man. Perhaps we men are being shaped to an idea in which we are not distinguished from other forms of being at all.

Again, if we could comprehend in its entirety the idea of which Praxiteles had only a partial intimation, we might find that it was, somehow, a single model for all creation, that it was not one of many models, each with a specific label—as "man," "dog," etc. My inclination is monist; I suppose the *Logos* to be indivisible; but for purposes of thought and expression one cannot escape the necessity of division.

2. *"Thus, according to Socrates, the human idea of beauty corresponds to a truth of nature. It represents the human apprehension of what is divine. The sculptor who expresses*

[1] E. W. F. Tomlin, *Great Philosophers of the East*, London, 1959, pp. 36ff. and 310.

119

it in a statue, although himself mortal, is expressing an eternal truth, a truth which existed before him and will remain after." This is what is meant by the conclusion of Keats's "Ode on a Grecian Urn": " 'Beauty is truth, truth beauty,'—that is all ye know on earth, and all ye need to know."

3. The doctrine of the *Logos* is not peculiar to one school of philosophy. It is in the "Memphite Drama," whose authors held that the material universe was thought incarnated; in the Babylonian tradition represented by the "Epic of Gilgamesh" (perhaps as early as 3000 B.C.); in Hebrew thought, where it is sometimes personified as Divine Wisdom; in the speculations of Heraclitus; and in Plato. It is in the Indian "Upanishads" (probably 800 to 500 B.C.), where the *Logos* has the name of "Brahman"; it is in the philosophy of Shankara, the Hindu, who lived about the eighth or ninth century A.D.; it is in Taoism and in Confucianism.[2] It is exemplified in the following passage from Thomas Aquinas: *"Est in intellectu divino veritas proprie et primo, in intellectu vero humano proprie quidem et secundario, in rebus autem improprie et secundario, quia non nisi in respectu ad alterutram duarum veritatum* [Truth is primarily proper to the divine understanding. It is secondarily proper to the human understanding. It exists in things only as being not proper to them and secondary, for it can be identified only in relation to its existence in either the divine or the human understanding]."[3]

Perhaps one could go so far as to say that the doctrine of the *Logos* is implicit in all philosophies that do not, like positivism, explicitly deny it.

SECTION 3

1. *"Any human observer is able to determine the behavior and the social organization proper to the honeybee; none can*

---

[2] See Tomlin, *op.cit.*, references in index.
[3] *Quaestiones disputatae*, VII: "De veritate," qu. I, art. IV, 8.

tell what is proper to himself." D. H. Lawrence once wrote: "If a man were as much a man as a lizard is a lizard, he would be more worth looking at."

2. The quatrain is from *The Poetical Works of Sir Henry Taylor*, London, 1864, Vol. III, p. 250.

3. The quotation is from Huxley's "The Uniqueness of Man," *Yale Review*, Vol. 28, p. 473, reprinted in a book of that title (London, 1941). Here Huxley expounds the thesis of this section, that only man has not yet completed his evolution.

4. My statement of Huxley's thesis is more absolute than the actuality would warrant. Evolution by natural selection must be an automatic response in every species to changes in its environment. If summers become cooler it will transpire that some bees are better adapted to the new temperature than others, and they will have the advantage over the others in reproducing their kind. The honeybee, however, has in large measure lost its earlier capacity for adaptation, in the sense that its individuals have come to represent a greater uniformity. It has arrived at its end, moreover, in the sense that it is quite completely adapted to its basic environment, which is relatively stable. Men represent a greater variety and, consequently, a greater range within which natural selection may operate. (As the biologists put it, they are distinguished by their polymorphism and polytypicism.) Furthermore, they are not nearly as well adapted, yet, to their basic environment.

SECTION 4

1. The association of beards, etc., with political allegiance in nineteenth-century France is taken from the *Souvenirs* of Maxime du Camp (Vol. I, p. 45) by C. H. C. Wright in his *The Background of Modern French Literature*, Boston, 1926, p. 141, footnote.

2. The quotation from Cicero is from *De Re Publica*, Book 3, XXII.

3. Since these chapters will hereafter be concerned so largely with political philosophy (although not exclusively), the following observations come best at this point.

Except in terms of the dual philosophy, there can be no meaning in literature, art, or music. A meadow with trees in it represents nothing in itself. The artist, however, sees in it a reflection of the *Logos*. He sees the invisible perfection behind the visible imperfection. It is an idea of this perfection that he brings out in his painting of the landscape, as Praxiteles brings out an idea of the perfection of the human form in his statue. When we look at the painting we see the idea behind it as we see the idea of the straight line when we look at the pencil-mark. Not having the sensitivity of the artist, we might not have seen such an idea if we had looked at the landscape directly. The painting brings it out, so that we are more likely to see it the next time we look at the landscape directly. It is in this sense that the artist teaches us to see.

In what is written about the meaning of music it is commoner to note that music is communication than to say what it communicates. To say that it communicates the composer's vision begs the question. What it communicates is a conception of the *Logos*, and this it is that moves us when we listen to it.

The dual philosophy explains not only art but the commonest kind of experience as well.

The anticipation of a pleasurable experience, and the memory of it, generally have a perfection that is lacking in the experience itself. This is disguised by the fact that the memory so quickly replaces the experience. Nevertheless, those who have made themselves self-conscious at the moment of experience have noted a disappointment. Various writers have observed that, pleasant as sexual experience may be, it is not as rapturous as the anticipation of it or, perhaps, as golden as the memory. The idea has a perfection which the realization lacks, and the realization itself is more pleasurable to the extent that the imagination is active throughout it. "Love," said Talleyrand in a memorable apothegm, "is a reality of the imagination."

It is not fanciful to attribute the remarkable power of Ernest Dowson's lyric, "*Non sum qualis eram . . .*" (with its refrain, "I have been faithful to thee, Cynara! in my fashion"), to its evocation of a contrast, familiar in all men's experience, between idea (here in the guise of a memory) and existential reality.

When I say that we live in two worlds at once, I mean to say that we do so at every instant of our waking and sleeping lives.

SECTION 5

1. The sentence from Paley occurs in *Works of Wm. Paley, D.D.*, London, 1825, Vol. IV, p. 477.

2. Similes, which may be true within the limits of what they are invoked to illuminate, may be misleading beyond those limits. The occasion of this observation is the comparison between the molecules, associated by common organization to make the blade of grass, and the French citizens, associated by common organization to make the French state. We shall see in Section 9 that the blade of grass belongs to a different order of being from the French state.

3. "*Associations by likeness . . . are matters of more or less.*" The individual particles of experience may be associated together by similarities more or less great, or they may be dissociated from one another by differences more or less great. The question whether the similarities or the differences are greater—whether, in other words, the individuals are more validly associated or dissociated—is not a question of objective fact but of subjective point of view. It is a question

123

of the scale in the mind against which the similarities or differences are measured. A mile is nothing in interstellar space; it is an appreciable distance for me to walk; it would be unthinkably enormous at the end of my nose. The distance from M to N appears greater in a close-up view than the distance from A to Z in a distant view. Comparing Americans and English in a view that does not extend beyond the two nations, I am impressed by the differences between them; comparing them in a view that includes Hottentots and Australian aborigines, I am impressed by the similarities.

Kant long ago noted that scholars tend to fall into two groups, those who follow the principle of "homogeneity" and those who follow the principle of "specification." "This distinction," he wrote, "manifests itself likewise in the habits of thought peculiar to natural philosophers, some of whom—the remarkably speculative heads—may be said to be hostile to heterogeneity in phenomena, and have their eyes always fixed on the unity of genera, while others—with a strong empirical tendency—aim unceasingly at the analysis of phenomena, and almost destroy in us the hope of ever being able to estimate the character of these according to general principles." He concluded that one "reasoner has at heart the interest of *diversity*—in accordance with the principle of specification; another, the interest of *unity*—in accordance with the principle of aggregation."[4]

It is pointless to ask whether the world as seen through a microscope or the world as seen through a telescope is the world as it really is. The experience of the earthworm and the experience of the eagle are, equally, experiences of reality. There is a distinction, however, in terms of meaningful experience. If the ultimate reality, which is the *Logos*, is a single order that comprehends all being, then the larger view will be more revealing of it than the smaller. Because the

[4] *Critique of Pure Reason*, translated by J. M. D. Meiklejohn, London, 1934, pp. 379-80, 386.

124

order of the universe is found in the association of its particles, all the great visions that have advanced human understanding have been those of minds that, to use Kant's language, were influenced more by the interest of unity. The greatness of an Einstein or of a Shakespeare is in the comprehensiveness of his vision.

The nobler and more meaningful view, in international relations, is that which reduces the differences between men and nations. (Cf. One, 6.)

4. *"The existence of the individual is absolute and unmistakable."* Within the limits of our concern here this is true. Among lower animals, however, and among plants, the isolation and identification of individuals may involve difficulties that at last put into question the whole concept of individuality as applied to them. Think, for example, of a ground creeper (like the common ivy, *Hedera helix*) that expands and perpetuates itself indefinitely by runners; that may be chopped up and still live and develop in its parts, which continue to expand and perpetuate themselves.

SECTION 6

1. *"... in terms of the dual philosophy, ideas are primary, the phenomena of the visible world being created in imitation of them."* This is true alike of the ideas that belong to the largely unknown *Logos* and those ideas of propriety, supposed to correspond to the *Logos*, that inhabit our minds. The idea of his Hermes existed in the mind of Praxiteles before the statue as the idea of light existed before there was light.

2. *"... the Aphrodite of Melos. ..."* This refers to the statue in the Louvre better known as "the Venus de Milo." While the Roman goddess Venus is closely identified with the Greek goddess Aphrodite, she has a somewhat different origin and therefore cannot be quite the same person. For

this and other reasons it seems preferable to give the Greek goddess her Greek identity.

3. "[*The statue of the American woman*] *is . . . a generalization. . . .*" It is a generalization only if there is reason to regard it as such. The simple observer may assume that, just as the field is in general green, so American women are in general that tall. A somewhat sophisticated observer, on the other hand, will have in mind that a height of five feet in the statue might mean that all the specimens measured were five feet tall or, equally well, that half were two feet tall and the other half eight feet tall. A truly sophisticated observer, however, will know that American women are never as short as two feet or as tall as eight. He will therefore surmise that five feet is a measure about which the individual measurements tend to cluster.[5]

4. The same nominal abstraction may be an idea of propriety and also a generalization. In the mind of a Frenchman, an idea of the typical Frenchman may be an idea of propriety which he imitates and also a generalization (however false) if he assumes that it represents the existential reality as it is. (In the mind of a German it might be an idea of what is propriety for Frenchmen, though not for Germans, who have other models to imitate.)

5. "*. . . we inhabit, at one and the same time, a real world and a nominal world.*" The pejorative term "nominal," to designate our abstract concepts, has been established in Western philosophy since the thirteenth century, when Albertus Magnus made it current. It is not quite adequate in its implication that our concepts, which are not real in themselves, are no more than names. They are visions more or less true, more or less false. They may be said, however, to stand in the same rough relation to realities as names do to things. Moreover, although the nominal element is not the only one

[5] I am indebted to Dr. H. L. Shapiro of the American Museum of Natural History, in whose office the statue stands, for information about it.

126

in our concepts, it is all-important in that it involves them in its own logic.[6]

6.

Real

1. LOGOS ←— *THIS*

THIS ⟶ is imperfectly represented by

2. EXISTENTIAL THINGS ←—*THIS*

is imperfectly represented by

Nominal

IDEAS OF PROPRIETY AND GENERALIZATIONS

THIS ⟶

The *Logos* is imperfectly represented by:
(a) *existential things* and the *generalizations* that, in turn, represent them imperfectly.
(b) *ideas of propriety* (also called *nominal ideas*).

SECTION 7

"The reason why sexual relations or intermarriage between Negroes and whites arouses particular passion among them is that it implies the future proliferation of Americans who do not conform to the idea which they are seeking to imitate."

[6] See One, 25.

127

The opponents of such miscegenation have not necessarily rationalized their opposition in these terms—although some have. Ideas of propriety and impropriety may be based on a logic of which those who hold them are unaware. The individual birds and beasts are generally attracted to their sexual partners by features that make for genetic strength in the progeny, even though they know nothing of genetic considerations. The instinctive abhorrence of incest throughout almost all mankind, and the behavior patterns by which it is averted in some other species, are not based on any knowledge of the genetic dangers that justify it.

It is virtually the rule among us men that our attitudes and opinions are based, at best, on an unconscious logic which we have to discover in ourselves *ex post facto* when required to give explanations.

SECTION 8

1. *"Where the state already exists it is moved to promote the development of a corresponding community within its jurisdiction...."* More precisely, those who act for the state are so moved.

2. The cases in which the state precedes the community, or in which the name precedes it, are commoner than one generally supposes.

Presumably the people of Panama, today, who boast that they are Panamanians, would be boasting that they were Colombians if the Government of Colombia, in 1903, had not provoked the Government of the United States into conniving at the separation from Colombia of what is now the sovereign state of Panama.

The argument may be made that the United States, too, was a state before it was a nation. In the beginning the people that were to form the American nation were Englishmen. These Englishmen were joined, over the years, by Irishmen,

Germans, Italians, Poles, and a number of other nationalities. All these people (in a word that is a paradox in itself) became "naturalized" as Americans. The default of an American nation as the condition precedent of the American state has always been felt by us as a weakness for which we have compensated by the anxious promotion of something called "Americanism." We have insisted on our distinct national identity the more fervently because of a doubt that it existed naturally; and by this insistence we have, at last, brought it into existence. We are a "naturalized" nation.

The French state appears to have existed before there was a French nation. By the beginning of the sixteenth century that state had emerged from the confusion which followed the disintegration of the Roman Empire as a kingdom with boundaries roughly corresponding to the boundaries of what, today, we call the French nation. But what it represented primarily was the area over which one man, and his successive heirs, were able to hold sway. It was not until the French Revolution, some three centuries later, that the existence of a French nation became manifest. And then a century would elapse, still, before the French language, cherished and promoted by the French Academy and by the Ministry of Public Instruction in Paris, became the language of the whole country.

Modern nationalism has, to some extent, been imposed on populations by a variety of psychological devices sponsored, in the first instance, by governments. The theory that the state is the people, representing the will of the people, has made this necessary. A government pretending to express the will of the people has to make the people (as well as itself) believe that this is so. To the extent that its policy does not represent the one national will of the theory, because such a will does not exist, the several wills of the actuality must be pressed to conform. Extreme examples of this may be found where even liberal states, going to war, are constrained to stigmatize and penalize as disloyalty any dissent from that policy.

The imposition of modern nationalism by the state has also responded to the theory by which the state justifies its sovereign independence, that it represents a people distinct by nature from every other people. The Irish Free State, having justified its separation from England on the ground that the Irish are a separate nation, finds this position weakened by the fact that the Irish speak the same language as the English. It is, consequently, moved to make every effort to replace English by an exclusive national language, which will show beyond question that the Irish constitute a separate nation. Here again, in some measure at least, the nation is consequent upon the state. The justification of self-determination is produced *ex post facto*.

The nominal theory that the people constitute a corporate entity with one will may be wide of the reality at first, but where that theory prevails a variety of social pressures will operate to promote consensus and eliminate dissent. If the masters of the state can develop sufficiently effective means for molding the will of the nation, imposing the consensus that appears convenient and eliminating dissent, then the result of using such means will be to validate the theory that the state represents the will of the nation. The identification of state and nation will be achieved, then, although by the reverse of the procedure that the authors of the popular revolution had had in mind. For they had postulated the pre-existence of a general will which would govern the state, whereas what has happened is that a pre-existing state has created a general will which remains under its government.

Today we still give the term "nation" priority over the term "sovereign state" in the vocabulary of international relations. We refer to "nationalism" rather than "statism." We have a community of "nations," organized as the "United Nations." In the conclusions reached at San Francisco in the spring of 1945 it was, we say, the "nations" or the "peoples" of the world expressing their common determination. In point of fact, however, it was sovereign states that were represented at San Francisco and it is sovereign states that are represented at meetings of the United Nations. These sovereign states may or may not be representative of nations; and where they are representative of nations, that may or may not be because they have the means to make up the minds of the nations they represent.

To qualify for admission to the international community today an entity has to be a sovereign state; but it does not have to be a nation and, in fact, nations as such are not eligible. This tends to be disguised by the convention according to which every sovereign state, today, is regarded as the spokesman of a nation.

The organization of the United Nations does not represent a triumph of internationalism so much as it represents the triumph of nationalism. It gives the nation-state a standing in the world, and a legitimacy, such as it never had before. The proclamation in its Charter of the principle of sovereign equality represents, in fact, an ultimate recognition of the personality of the nation-state.

When one studies the membership of the United Nations today, it becomes apparent that the nation-state is not the natural phenomenon which, under the influence of the nineteenth-century nationalists, we had assumed it to be. The ambiguity in the national character of most of the United Nations would be apparent to us if they did not happen to exist as sovereign states that have clothed themselves in the legendry of nationalism. The prior existence of the state, in the case of the majority of members, shows to what an extent nations, in our day, are artificial products rather than natural growths.[6a]

[6a] For an important qualification of the above observations, see Two, 33, 6.

SECTION 9

1. *"The question implicit in political theory from the beginning has been: What is the political organization proper to man as a matter of nature?"* The typical political theorist in any age has accepted the features of his passing environment as normal and forever established, like the organization of the hive. But no sooner has he made this assumption than it has been invalidated by a new revolution, by breakdown and renewed experiment. No sooner had Aristotle assumed that the sovereign city-state was nature's fundamental unit than his pupil, Alexander, proceeded to gather the city-states which he had known into one centrally governed empire, the prototype of the approaching Roman Empire. Thomas Aquinas and Dante assumed a universal Christian empire under divine control at a time when Christendom, with its political inheritance from Rome, was about to break up into a multitude of sovereign states. John Locke took the Whig polity produced by the Revolution of 1688 as his model of human propriety.[7] Rousseau idealized the republican city of which he was a native. Karl Marx, looking at the class struggle that produced the revolutions of 1848, extrapolated it to the dimensions of all history: there had always been an exploited class, he thought, moving toward a revolution against an exploiter class; and this would continue until the drama of history came to an end, at last, in a classless society as unchanging as that of the bees. Today, living in an increasingly uniform and regimented world, it is easy to see the beehive as the model of man's future. Tomorrow the prospect may be something else again.

People naturally believe that the way of life to which they have been brought up is, basically, the only proper way of

---

[7] His *Two Treatises of Government* were begun before 1688 although published after. They and the Revolution represent the same idea of propriety, current at the time. The idea represented by the Stuart monarchy had become obsolete.

life. It is what God or nature intended. They have inherited it from their ancestors and expect to pass it on to their descendants, and they hope that all the world will eventually inherit it.

This sense of propriety and this conservative tendency, which contribute to the individual's feeling of personal security, lead to a wishful exaggeration of every culture's stability. Germans, to the extent that they are nationalistic, find it easy to pride themselves on an unbroken cultural heritage from the days chronicled by Tacitus, if not from the days of Siegfried and the Nibelungen; Italians may see themselves as carrying on the traditions of Roman culture; Greeks may identify their culture with that of Periclean Athens; and modern Jews may feel that they are perpetuating the culture of the pastoral nomads who followed Moses out of Egypt. In fact, however, while the fundamentals of a culture have a quality of persistence that is real, cultures change more rapidly than we like to admit; and even the cultural history of China, which seems the most stable of all, seems less stable the more closely it is examined. Any modern Jew who found himself back with the company of Moses might quickly come to regard that company as savages of another species. The cultural changes which those of us who have lived long enough have seen in our own countries and within our own lifetime alone are impressive; and not only in mechanical or technological change, but in the cast of men's minds as well.

2. *"From Hobbes to Rousseau, they postulated a state of nature from which mankind had departed when it undertook to establish governments and the rule of law."* This is clearly true of the Rousseau who wrote the *Discourse on the Origins of Inequality among Men* (1755). It is not as clearly true of the Rousseau who wrote the *Social Contract* (1762). This later Rousseau, anticipating the nationalists of the nineteenth century, had become increasingly entranced by his vision of an organized society as an idea of propriety. Since one does

not gain credit for an idea of propriety by saying that it is not proper to nature, we hear little in the *Social Contract* of how artificial any organized society must be. Still, in Book III, Chapter XI, Rousseau writes: "The constitution of a man is a work of nature; that of the State is a work of art." Rousseau's successors in the nineteenth century (Fichte and Mazzini, for example) will argue that the organized state responds to the intention of God, of nature, or of history.

3. *"The myth of social contract, which Rousseau recognized as such. . . ."* In the fourth paragraph of the Preface to his *Discourse on the Origins of Inequality among Men*, referring to the original state of nature, Rousseau writes: ". . . it is not a light undertaking to distinguish what is primordial [*originaire*] and what artificial in human nature as it is today, and to know well a state that no longer exists, that perhaps never did exist, that probably never will exist, but of which it is still necessary to have sound notions, in order to have a sound understanding of our present state." If the state of nature never existed, then there never was an actual social contract by which our ancestors departed from it. The social contract is a myth to explain society. Rousseau is saying, in effect, that men find themselves in a state of mutual obligation, in contractual relations with one another, as if they actually had, at some time, drawn up and concluded a formal contract.

4. *"In every organized society there must be a sovereign from whom decisions flow, whether that sovereign is a man or an abstraction."* The sovereign may be a nominal abstraction ("the people," conceived as a corporate person); it may be a nominal abstraction embodied in an individual person (the British crown, from which decisions nominally flow); or it may be an individual person thought to be sovereign in his own right rather than by virtue of his office (what Max Weber called the charismatic leader—Hitler, for example).

5. *"As so many fragments ensuing upon the break-up of the universal mediaeval empire...."*

The Roman Empire, like the Chinese, represented an idea of propriety that included universalism. Nominally, Rome ruled the entire world. When the Roman order fell into anarchy, and when finally there was no longer a Roman emperor (if one excepts the nominal claim that the rulers of Byzantium sustained into the fifteenth century), the idea persisted still. It represented the norm, the normal condition of affairs in the minds of men. The prevailing anarchy appeared as only a temporary lapse from this norm. Charlemagne made a notable attempt to re-establish normality. In the Holy Roman Empire, Rome continued a nominal existence until 1806, when Napoleon put an end to it. It survives nominally still today, in the institution of the papacy.

Beginning with the Renaissance and Reformation, the normative idea of dynastic states—or of national states or of national churches—was in conflict for centuries with the normative idea of the Roman Empire. The conflict goes on still today, although now in a highly modified and limited form.

6. *"... 'the most Serene and most Potent Princess Anne, by the Grace of God, Queen of Great Britain, France, and Ireland.' ..."*

Until the Peace of Amiens in 1802, British monarchs nominally included France among the countries under their rule, although they had not actively asserted a claim to France since The Hundred Years' War. The genius of British government has always been to accept the discrepancy between the nominal and the real, even at a sacrifice of logic which the French, for example, would find it difficult to make. The British are not disturbed by the illogic of a church that, nominally, is at once "Anglo-" and "catholic." They are not disturbed by the illogic of a situation in which the Queen, when she crosses the border from England to Scotland, abruptly becomes converted to Presbyterianism, becoming reconverted to Anglocatholicism when she recrosses it in the opposite direction. The typically British solution to the problems of politics is to trade the real for the nominal and the nominal for the real, sacrificing nothing more than logic.

7. *"At San Francisco in 1945 sixty individual persons, vested with the authority of as many sovereign states, some of them what we call dictatorships and a few what we call liberal democracies, drew up and agreed upon a document that begins: 'We, the peoples of the United Nations ...'"*

The present Constitution of Japan, drawn up by the foreign military authorities who were occupying Japan as a defeated enemy, and promulgated while they were still in occupation, begins: "We, the Japanese people ... do proclaim the sovereignty of the people's will and do ordain and establish this Constitution. ..." Here the occupation authorities were creating a nominal state of affairs that would tend to mold the real state of affairs after they had withdrawn.

SECTION 10

The passage from Rousseau appears in the *Social Contract*, Book II, Chapter I.

SECTION 11

1. *"What Rousseau meant by the general will was something quite different from that occasional predominance of voices with which we identified it in the last section."*

The basic concept in Rousseau is of something that corresponds to what we have called "the *Logos*." It is the concept of an *a priori* propriety, of an absolute rightness not to be distinguished from the public good. It is justice and the self-interest of society in one.

Some philosophers in the past had chosen to call this "the will of God." Some had chosen to call it "the law of nature."

Rousseau, unfortunately, chooses to call it "the general will," on the grounds that all members of society will it in principle. His fatal first step, then, is to call his basic concept something other than what it is in itself, to name it by something that pertains to it only accidentally.

From the outset he is involved in the consequent paradoxes. If he had called his basic concept "the right," there would have been no paradox in noting that the will of the people, as expressed in an assembly or a plebiscite, might not correspond to it. There is a paradox, however, in noting that the will of the people may not correspond to "the general will."

Presumably Rousseau gets himself into this position because he wishes to make an argument for popular sovereignty. If the right is to prevail, and if the people is to be sovereign as well, then the right must be identified with the will of the people. But the people may will what is wrong. To deal with the problem this poses, a distinction must be made between the will of the people when it is infallibly right and the will of the people when it is wrong. This Rousseau does by distinguishing "the general will" from "the will of all." "The general will," he tells us, "is always right and tends always to the public good; but it does not follow that the deliberations of the people always have the same rectitude. . . . There is often a great difference between the will of all and the general will."[6b] (The general will is infallibly right because it is by definition the will that has the prevalence of the right as its object.)

The distinction between the will of all and the general will is not altogether spurious. If, for example, I am asked what my will is with respect to the level of taxation, I may reply that I favor a lower level. If, then, I am also asked what my will is with respect to the abstract question whether the government should always do what is right, I shall say my will is that it should. My two responses will conflict, however,

[6b] *Du Contrat Social*, Book II, Chapter III.

137

if what is right is that the level of taxation should not be lowered. According to Rousseau's distinction, my response to the first question represents my particular will (which is individual and therefore anti-social), while my response to the second represents my participation in the general will. It is quite possible, in these terms, that the unanimous will of all (the aggregate of all individual wills) might be for lower taxes while the general will was for higher taxes. Here is a logical distinction on the basis of which one may reconcile the prevalence of right with the dogma of popular sovereignty. Popular sovereignty expresses itself, not in the will of all, but in the general will.

The general will, however, is for something that may be unknown to the people: namely, whatever is right.

This brings us face to face with the question that has been lurking between the lines all along: How does one know what is right? How does one know what this unknown object of the general will is? How, to use Rousseau's compressed terminology, does one know what the general will is?

The will of all refers to existential reality. One can find out what it is by consulting that reality. One can call the people together and ask for a show of hands, or one can hold a plebiscite. But the general will (i.e., the object of the general will) belongs to what we have called the *Logos*. It does not belong to existential reality, so that we have no reason to believe that we could determine what it was by consulting that reality.

Here we confront what we have recognized to be the dilemma of mankind: that we don't know the *Logos*, that we don't know what constitutes human propriety.

This did not seem to present such a difficulty to philosophers before Hume (who was Rousseau's contemporary) as it does to us. Ever since Cicero it had been widely believed that what was right could be known by the right operation of human reason. In the eighteenth century it was generally held that basic truths were self-evident to properly qualified men. Rousseau shared this view. What was right would always be self-evident to any person who was well-intentioned and sufficiently informed. And, once the people had themselves been made well-intentioned and sufficiently informed, then it would be self-evident to them, too.

Does this, then, solve the problem?

Not quite. After all, Rousseau's distinction between the general will and the will of all is based on a recognition of the fact that an appreciable proportion of the people is not yet well-intentioned and informed. This leaves the problem in being, at least for a transitional period until the people has become well-intentioned and informed. In that transitional period the only possible solution is for a qualified individual or individuals to assume the responsibility of making the general will prevail.

In his chapter on "The Legislator"[8] Rousseau sets forth this responsibility, what it entails, and the qualifications needed by whoever assumes it. But here a difficulty arises. If one could be sure that the Legislator spoke for the general will, which is the expression of the people's sovereignty, he would only be imposing the sovereignty of the people by forcing the people to obey it. This has been Rousseau's logic right along. In Book I, Chapter VII, he writes: "Whoever refuses to obey the general will shall be constrained by the whole body: which is merely to say that he shall be forced to be free." It follows that, if the Legislator speaks for the general will, freedom itself requires that all be constrained to obey him.

The difficulty is that, as it now transpires, one cannot be sure he does speak for the general will. "One can never be sure," says Rousseau, "that an individual will conforms to the general will until after it has been submitted to the free suffrage of the people."

[8] Book II, Chapter VII.

We have been imprisoned, at last, in a circular argument, which has brought us back to seeking the general will in the suffrage of the people. The people must vote on what it is. But this also brings us back to the question: how can we make sure that their vote will not represent the will of all rather than the general will?

Rousseau tries to meet the difficulty by making conditions. The issues put to the vote should be few and general. The voter must be asked to vote, not for what he wills as an individual, but for what he believes the general will to be.

There are other conditions, too. All the members of the community must participate in the voting. There may be no associations among the voters, no subcommunities within the community of the whole, no political parties. In fact, assurance of deriving the general will from popular deliberation would be conditional upon a state of affairs in which, "when the sufficiently informed people deliberated, the Citizens had no communication among themselves. . . ."[9] Finally, the whole thing is unlikely to work on a scale larger than that of the city-state. (Rousseau was thinking of Sparta, of Rome, and of his native Geneva, which in his day had a population of some twenty thousand.)

Still we face the issue of the votes that represent individual wills, the votes of the misled. What about them?

In the third chapter of Book II Rousseau argues that the votes of those who are expressing merely their own individual wills must, by some law of probability not made apparent to the reader, nullify one another by falling equally on the two respective sides of any issue. What remains will then represent the proper votes, the majority of which will, in turn, represent the general will.

Here is the answer, the best that can be given.

The reader is not convinced, and there is internal evidence that Rousseau is not quite convinced either. Doubts pile up

[9] Book II, Chapter III.

that any procedure for surely identifying what is right will work this side of the kingdom of heaven.

But Rousseau never faces this dilemma. The basic self-evidence of what is right remains a tacit assumption under all his thought, even though he comes to such a lame conclusion in devising a procedure for its public determination. So at last one is compelled to ask the question implicit in the assumption itself. If what is right is known, why insist on calling it a general will? Why insist on popular sovereignty? Why bother about a majority vote? What is right is right, and so it does not matter whether we call it the general will or the will of McPherson's cow. It is the right thing to do in any case.

2. *"From the beginning, all thinkers who have taken the long view have meant something different [from an occasional predominance of voices] by [the general will]."*

Edmund Burke wrote that "society" or "the state" (he used the terms interchangeably) is a partnership "not only between those who are living, but between those who are living, those who are dead, and those who are to be born. Each contract of each particular state is but a clause in the great primeval contract of eternal society, linking the lower with the higher natures, connecting the visible and invisible world, according to a fixed compact sanctioned by the inviolable oath which holds all physical and all moral natures, each in their appointed place."[10]

3. The citation of Lippmann is from *The Public Philosophy*, Boston, 1955, pp. 31-36.

4. Rousseau's statement that the public "must be taught to know what it wills" is in the *Social Contract*, Book II, Chapter VI.

5. Marx's statement is in Karl Marx and Friedrich Engels, *Historisch-Kritische Gesamtausgabe: Werke, Schriften,*

---

[10] *Reflections on the Revolution in France*, London, 1950, p. 106.

Briefe, Marx-Engels Archiv, Verlagsgesellschaft M. B. H., Frankfurt a. M., 1927, I, 1, p. 575.

SECTION 12

1. *"The English and Americans preferred the procedure of counting noses to find a consensus and then simplifying the result by eliminating minority opinions from the final picture."* They also, by various devices, tempered this procedure to protect the permanent community, which includes unborn generations, against transient majorities moved by wayward impulses. The Constitution of the United States is full of such devices, exemplified by the procedure for amending it and by the two-thirds rule on consent to the ratification of treaties in the Senate.

2. Roosevelt's statement was in a speech at Spokane, Washington, May 26, 1903.

3. Acton's well known dictum, in a letter to Dr. Creighton, was: "Power tends to corrupt and absolute power corrupts absolutely. Great men are almost always bad men. . . ."[11] Lord Acton, who dedicated his life to the unaccomplished task of writing a history of freedom (which has been called "the greatest book never written"), proved incapable of writing a book. He had the gift, however, of saying more in one sentence than other writers could say in volumes. He summed up much of what is said in this section (as well as in Two, 9, *1*, and Two, 25, *4*) in one of his pregnant sentences: "The history of institutions is often a history of deception and illusions; for their virtue depends on the ideas that produce and on the spirit that preserves them, and the form may remain unaltered when the substance has passed away."[12]

[11] *Essays on Freedom and Power*, Boston, 1949, p. 364.
[12] Essay on "The History of Freedom in Antiquity," *op.cit.*, p. 31.

SECTION 13

1. *"Both the liberal and Jacobin procedures are based on the premise that, among the forms of being in the existential world, there is a personal entity called 'the people.' . . . Nationalists conceive of it as plural, as represented by many 'peoples' or 'nations.'"*

"In the history of the world," said the nationalist, Hegel, "the individuals we have to do with are Peoples."[13]

2. The quotation from Rousseau occurs in the *Social Contract*, Book II, Chapter VII.

3. *"The modern psychological techniques called 'brainwashing' respond to this need [i.e., the need to transform human nature]."*

In his article on *Political Economy* Rousseau says: "the most absolute authority is that which penetrates to the interior of a man and exerts itself not less on his will than on his actions. It is certain that men are, in the long run, what governments make them." He had just finished saying that, "if it is good to know how to employ men as they are, it is far better still to transform them into what one needs them to be."[14]

4. *"Jacobinism . . . takes an* a priori *logic as its point of departure and insists on the conformity of existential circumstances."*

Rousseau, who was imagining a Utopia more than he was planning a society to be established in actuality, saw the necessity of such conformity but lacked the ruthlessness of his later followers to insist on it. While he said that each individual must be transformed, that his proper faculties must be replaced by faculties foreign to him, it is doubtful that he expected such a task to be undertaken in fact.

This was not the case with Marx, and the fact that it was

---

[13] *The Philosophy of History*, trans. J. Sibrée, New York, 1944, p. 14 (quoted by Bowle, *Politics and Opinion*, London, 1954, p. 45).

[14] Text included in edition of *Du Contrat Social*, Paris, 1943, p. 232.

not may represent his true significance as a prophet of our times. The classical political theorists had been concerned with the problem of reconciling the individual diversity of mankind, of fitting the social structure to men as they were. Marx fitted human nature to the social structure instead. Where others had derived the organization of society from the nature of man, he derived the nature of man from the organization of society.

Marx and Engels maintained that "the premises with which we begin are not arbitrary, not dogmas but real premises from which one can derive abstractions only in the imagination. They are the real individuals, their actions and the material conditions of their lives, alike those that already exist and those produced by their own action. These premises, consequently, are verifiable by purely empirical procedures."[15] This claim represents a paradox that would surely have delighted the author of *Alice in Wonderland*. Marx was captivated by the abstract idea of empiricism, but the practice remained unknown to him. He lived so exclusively in the world of ideas that he was unable to recognize, by empirical evidence, his lack of empiricism. This applies, as well, to the present claims of Marxist-Leninist dogma to be a science.

Marx was not a student of men as flesh-and-blood creatures. He was at home only with theoretical abstractions. The basic human entity, for him, was not the individual but the class. The individual's tastes, opinions, and attitudes were essentially nothing more than functions of the social class to which he belonged. This implies that the tastes, opinions, and attitudes of every member of a class are bound to be essentially identical with those of every other member. Marx assumed, for example, that there were no essential national or cultural differences among the world's proletariat. Here was the image of the beehive society. If the empirical facts,

[15] *Marx-Engels Gesamtausgabe*, Abteilung I, Band 5: "Die Deutsche Ideologie," 1845-46, Marx-Engels Verlag G. M. B. H., Berlin, 1932, p. 10.

the existential facts, contradicted it, if in actuality some members of the proletariat were different from others, then the facts were subject to correction by an intellectual élite organized as the Party. If some proletarians did not think as all proletarians were supposed to think, according to the doctrine, that must be because they had been drugged by their exploiters—seduced by religion ("the opium of the people"), misled by bourgeois idealism or sentimentalism. They would therefore have to be awakened to a proper class-consciousness, brought to understand what their true views were and what it was they wanted. The mission of the intellectual élite was to make them "conscious" where they were still unconscious.

According to this theory, the standardized man, a statistic in the mass, a carbon-copy of every other man, devoid of individual differences, represented the normal and proper condition of human society. Individual variation was a disease to be cured—by propaganda, by indoctrination, by the treatment accorded Pavlov's dog, by brainwashing. The facts would have to be made to fit the Marxian abstraction. If the proletariat was not in actuality what Karl Marx, isolated in the reading-room of the British Museum, had thought it was, then it would have to be made so.[16]

Marx's significance as a prophet is that he here provided a complete theoretical answer to the basic political dilemma of the mass society, of the state based on "the will" of multitudes. How is order and harmony to be maintained in a crowded industrial society of a hundred million or more individuals, no two of whom are quite alike, all of whom can

[16] Marx and Engels, after outlining the history of class-struggle to the point where the proletarian class is born, refer to that class as composed of "the majority of the members of the society . . . from which arises the consciousness of the necessity of a radical revolution, a consciousness that is the Communist consciousness and can arise as well in the other classes, thanks to the situation of this class." However, he adds, "a massive transformation of men is necessary for the mass creation of this Communist consciousness. . . ." *Op.cit.*, pp. 59-60.

claim a share in the government? The Marxist answer was to make them all alike, to rebuild them according to a standardized model (an idea of propriety). When every member of the state is identical with every other, the view of one will be the view of all; and it will no longer make any difference how many there are. No one will have to puzzle over majorities or minorities, over the problems of getting a consensus, over the crystallization of a general will on this issue or that. Unanimity will exist on the largest as on the smallest scale. If the bed of Procrustes does not fit men as they are, let it be the men who are made over. The absoluteness and the simplicity of this solution may explain the real strength of Marxism. Liberal philosophers, fussing over how to adapt one bed to individuals of so many individual shapes, have been able to produce nothing comparable. If it does nothing else, it provides a rationale for the most complete tyranny.

This is the end of that process whereby the people were liberated from the kings and the power of the kings handed over to them.

5. *"So liberalism compromises the purity of the concept in order to provide for the rights of dissenting individuals and minorities."*

Politics have to do with both worlds, the existential and the ideal. The problem is to take both into account and give each its due. The liberal tradition concerns itself with the existential reality of the individual in a way that the Jacobin tradition does not. Its premise is that the highest values reside in the individual as such, and are inseparable from him. It is the individual who has been cast in the image of his Maker, not the nation, or the state, or society. The soul, the spark of divinity, the faculty of reason—whatever one chooses to call it—is inherent in each one and cannot be abstracted.

This liberal tradition stems from the Judaic-Christian tradition as it developed, at last, under the transforming impact of Greek thought. The primitive god of the Penta-

146

teuch had condemned men collectively; but the salvation from this corporate doom which Jesus offered to a more sophisticated age was individual by individual. There is no suggestion in Christian doctrine that the souls of communities will be the subjects of the Last Judgment. Even Socrates and Plato thought in these terms. If the ideal community outlined in the *Republic* makes the individual subservient to an authoritarian state, this is because the state, in turn, is under the government of philosophers who alone can save him from the corruption into which he would otherwise fall, who alone can lead him to his individual salvation. But the good that resides in the individual is still primary. In the *Phaedo* Socrates is calm and clear in his belief that the state, though it may do what it wants to his body, cannot touch his soul, which is the ultimate good.

The men who represent the Jacobin-Marxist tradition, beginning with Rousseau, have been reformers concerned with the welfare of mankind. Typically, however, they have not been humanitarian, they have not been sensitive to the suffering or even the existence of individual human beings. A distinguished left-wing reformer of our times, in the course of a visit to a backward country, had his attention drawn to a little knot of people on the verge of starvation. He looked at them for a moment unseeing, then turned away. "Oh," he said, "the problem is so much bigger than just this!"—whereupon he proceeded to cite statistics of calory-intake per thousand of population. Rousseau, concerned with the education of mankind, was indifferent to that of his own children. A character in one of Edna St. Vincent Millay's plays says: "I am a philanthropist. I love humanity, but I hate people."

Here is a psychological type that has become increasingly predominant in modern times. In the Marxist-Leninist tradition, the humanitarianism of the Christian tradition is frankly denigrated as "bourgeois sentimentality." This explains the

147

paradox posed by cruelties practiced on the people in the name of the popular welfare.

6. *"The tension between liberalism of the left and liberalism of the right has existed since the beginning of the democratic revolution."*

From the eighteenth century to our present day, the tendency has been for liberal society and the predominant thinking among liberals to move slowly but rather steadily toward the left. All the compromises with majority rule, all the safeguards against it—such as limited suffrage, indirect election, provisions for decision by more than simple majorities, independence of the judiciary, the constitutional limitation of the power of governments over citizens—all these have tended to weaken or succumb. Mass public opinion has tended to be an ever more controlling factor. The theory of representative government set forth by Burke in his address to the electors of Bristol, that an elected official should exercise his own unfettered judgment on the issues that come before him, has given way before the theory that an elected official should subordinate his judgment to the consensus of his constituents.

The quasi-Jacobin or leftist liberal position has had an advantage from the first in its simplicity; in its tendency to bear out the assumption of the revolution that "the people" constitute a corporate entity which embodies virtue; in the support it gives the concept of the two species, which may easily be identified as the majority and the minority; and in its popular appeal (the candidate who proclaims his faith in "the people" is more likely to win the election than the one who avows his distrust of the mob). As the power of the state has passed from the hands of those who are conscious of constituting a minority into the hands of those who are conscious of constituting a majority, the protection of minorities and of non-conformity as a right has found its advocates less powerful. While all of us are members of innumerable minorities, we are inclined to minimize such membership; and it has not always been clear to those of us who are able to identify ourselves with the increasingly powerful majority why what is good enough for that majority should not be good enough for anyone. The notion of an élite is repugnant. So we see what is perhaps a natural cycle of liberal democracy, from minority rights to majority rule and, at last, to a demagogic authoritarianism that embodies the Jacobin concept of the two species: "the people" and "the enemies of the people."

This natural tendency (illustrated in the history of ancient Athens and of the Roman Republic) has been reinforced by the demographic and sociological consequences of the scientific and technological revolutions which have occurred since the eighteenth century. Mass-production industry, which employs labor in masses rather than as unique individuals, requires an approximation to machine-standardization in employees who are conceived of as payroll-statistics. The multiplication of populations as a result of science's prolongation of human life and reduction of infant mortality has crowded people together and promoted mass production of the facilities for living, so that the diversity of environments has been reduced. The movement of people from the countryside into the great new cities, besides crowding them together, has subjected them to an artificial environment that lacks the breadth and variety of nature. Radio and television have greatly extended the area over which a single influence can operate on the minds of men. As private and public enterprises have grown larger, and as the problems of administration have grown more extensive and complicated, great bureaucracies have developed which depend for their functioning on conformity within their ranks. The problem of achieving widespread consensus as the basis for decision and action—within the governmental bureaucracies, among the various branches of government, and among

149

millions of voters—has required the elimination of those distinguished minds that, inevitably, are disruptive of the process of achieving consensus at the only level at which it can be achieved, the level of the common mind. This was stated with a commendable candor by a management consultant, Dr. Robert McMurray: "Too much intelligence," he said, "is a handicap for day-to-day management because it hinders conformity and acceptance."[17]

All this amounts to saying that the physical and economic conditions of the hive tend, eventually, to produce the social conditions of the hive. One could conceive of a day in which the Marxian procedure of deriving human nature from the organization of society, rather than the other way around, was justified by the facts.

Under such circumstances as these, science and technology have been developing, in the Western democracies as in the Communist states, some formidable instruments for producing the mass mind. Television is, perhaps, the most obvious of these; but it is only one. Modern advertising, supported by vast expenditures and allied with psychological science, has increasingly mastered the principle of the conditioned reflex to the point where it can be confident of being able to decide the majority choice with respect to a broad range of subjects. Education, allied with psychiatry and sociology (and about to be allied with television), has been addressing itself increasingly to the production of "well-adjusted" rather than distinguished graduates. The "well-adjusted" are those who conform easily, those who can identify themselves with the common mind. All these developments are directed toward the establishment of undisputed majority rule by the elimination of minorities.

We should be mistaken, then, if we supposed that the Jacobin solution of the modern political dilemma was confined to the Communist countries. It has always had a power-

---

[17] Quoted by *The Observer*, London, December 21, 1958, p. 10.

ful appeal in the Western democracies, especially in the great cities that dominate them, where the name of Marx has had much of the magic quality which it has in the Communist countries. And in the newly liberated colonial countries the Jacobin-Marxist version of the concept of the two species has cast the ex-colonials as "the people," their former rulers as "the enemies of the people." The Marxist legend has had an appeal, under all these conditions, with which the philosophy of a Locke or a Burke could not compete.

All these considerations, so adverse to the future of liberalism, might give those who cherish the value of the individual grounds for despair. Such despair may be justified, but for myself I cannot accept it. While history has, as yet, provided inadequate evidence of what transformations the Jacobin state can produce in the individual, such evidence as it has produced bears out an aphorism of Mr. Bertram Wolfe, that "as soon as the screws are loosened men tend to spring back into human shape."

SECTION 14

1. Without attempting to draw a line between mythology and religion, we may note the transformation of any people's gods and heroes in the long course of its development. One character may, in the course of time, divide into several; or two merge into one, as Saint Nicholas merged into Father Christmas. A god or hero may change completely in time, perhaps coming progressively closer to the *Logos* (which is God).

The conception that prevails today of an omnipotent, an omniscient, and a largely unknowable God is the product of a radical evolution from the far different conception originally represented by Yahweh in the Pentateuch. As the passage from Genesis shows, Yahweh was neither omniscient nor infallible. When he wanted to know what was happening on earth, he had to walk about it with his own two legs, seeing with his own two eyes. He was capable of doing in anger what he would later repent of having done.

According to our most ancient tradition, the division of mankind into mutually opposed nations was a consequence of the hostility aroused in Yahweh after Adam's disobedience. For "the Lord was sorry that he had made man on the earth." Man, driven from Paradise, eventually found himself a hunted creature, not merely deprived of Yahweh's paternal care but subject to his embittered enmity. Only through exceptional favor to Noah as an individual was man allowed to survive at all. But the children of Noah had to fend for themselves; they had to make their own way on the earth.

In these circumstances they did better than Yahweh had anticipated. Having all "one language and few words," they were able to work together to build a common civilization. This alarmed Yahweh, when at last he came down to see what they were up to. "'Behold [he said], they are one people, and they have all one language, and this is only the beginning of what they will do; and nothing that they propose to do will now be impossible for them. Come, let us go down, and there confuse their language, that they may not understand one another's speech.' So Yahweh scattered them abroad from there over the face of all the earth, and they left off building the city."

Here, in the eleventh chapter of Genesis, is the beginning of international relations. Up to this point there had been no Jews, no Egyptians, no Philistines; no Frenchmen, Russians, or Chinese; no Moslems, no Hindus; no Ural-Altaic or Aryan languages. But from now on all is confusion and cross-purposes.

If we understand Yahweh as a being who had his own needs, and who was frustrated in their fulfillment, we may feel a certain sympathy for him. Man's failure is his failure too. He had created the heavens and earth; he had created

152

the living creatures according to their kinds; and last of all he had created man—in his image, after his likeness. Then man had failed him; and in this failure not only man was lost, Yahweh's single, universal realm was lost as well. In driving his own subjects away and in scattering them abroad he had broken up what had once been his own kingdom. But his need for subjects is manifest throughout this history. That is why Noah was saved. From the eleventh chapter on, we see Yahweh trying to establish, among the scattered nations of mankind, one nation that shall be his own. He chooses Abraham to be the father of such a nation; and he chooses Abraham's grandson, Jacob, to be its founder.

One of Yahweh's problems, after the dispersal from Babel, is that for the first time he has to contend with rival gods who have proliferated upon the earth now that its integrity has been lost. When one people gives way to many nations, monotheism gives way to polytheism.

The text makes it clear that the original authors of much of the Old Testament regarded the god of the Children of Israel as only one among a number of competing tribal gods. In the original Hebrew he was identified by a proper name, a name that has been commonly rendered as "Yahweh" or as "Jehovah." The King James translators followed a long-established precedent in substituting "the Lord" or sometimes "God" for this proper name. The editors of the Revised Standard Version have justified their continuance of this practice on the grounds that "the use of any proper name for the one and only God, as though there were other gods from whom He had to be distinguished, was discontinued in Judaism before the Christian era and is entirely inappropriate for the universal faith of the Christian Church."[18]

The religion of the most ancient Jews was not monotheistic but monolatrous: they believed in the existence of many

---

[18] In quoting from the Revised Standard Version I have restored the original, in most cases, to the extent of substituting "Yahweh" for "the Lord."

gods but worshipped only one of them, their own national god, Yahweh.[19] The monolatry of the ancient Jews gave way to monotheism gradually in the course of their development, although traces of it remain even today in the remnant of the belief that the one and only God is also a national god in the sense that the Jewish nation is his chosen instrument.

Yahweh's chief preoccupation, after the dispersal from Babel, is with the competition of rival gods, who hem him in and threaten his jurisdiction. He is constantly fighting to hold his own, while the children of Israel are constantly tempted to escape the severities of his rule by seeking the protection of his rivals.[20]

Having broken the world up into mutually opposed nations in the eleventh chapter of Genesis, Yahweh becomes an exclusive nationalist himself. Only his own people exist for him as objects of his care, of his moral responsibility, of justice, or of what we call humanitarian concern. He is not aware of the people of other nations, the people of rival gods, as being human too—capable of suffering and grief, of love for one another, of attachment to their homes, having a claim to justice and to mercy. One ought not to be more disturbed by Yahweh's foibles than by the peccadilloes of Zeus. He is like Zeus in lacking that omniscience and omnipotence which Jews and Christians today associate with the one and only God.

2. Where the concept of the corporate person has consequences that involve indiscriminate human suffering there have always been individuals like Abraham who experience sudden doubts about it. Though such an individual may accept the statement that Sodom has sinned, as soon as that

---

[19] Cf. Rabbi Isidore Epstein, *Judaism*, London, 1959, p. 55; and Dean William R. Inge, *Every Man's Bible*, New York, 1931, pp. xiii-xiv. "Who is like thee, O Yahweh, among the gods?" Moses and the people of Israel sing in Exodus 15:11.
[20] Cf. The Book of Jonah.

statement is followed by the proposition that Sodom be destroyed the concept of the corporate person disintegrates in his mind, giving way to the more vivid image of flesh-and-blood individuals, old men and young men, mothers and their children, boys and girls playing in the streets, infants sleeping or infants crying. It is on them that the punishment will fall. It is they who will feel the agony. Sodom is an abstraction and cannot be made to suffer as such. When suffering is involved an Abraham suddenly perceives who it is that, in reality, will do the suffering. Then, right or wrong, he takes it upon himself to speak.

The trouble that Abraham felt has expressed itself repeatedly through the generations. When King David sinned against Yahweh by taking a census of Israel, Yahweh sent a pestilence, "and there fell seventy thousand men of Israel. And Yahweh sent the angel to Jerusalem to destroy it. . . . And David lifted his eyes and saw the angel of Yahweh standing between earth and heaven, and in his hand a drawn sword stretched out over Jerusalem. Then David . . . said to Yahweh, 'Was it not I who gave command to number the people? It is I who have sinned and done very wickedly. But these sheep, what have they done? Let thy hand, I pray thee, O Yahweh my god, be against me and against my father's house; but let not the plague be upon thy people.' "

The most prolonged and profound debate over the concept of collective guilt has been occasioned by the doctrine of original sin in Christian theology, a doctrine that casts the whole of mankind in the role of Sodom. According to it, all men are guilty of Adam's disobedience. This sin, which is upon the heads of all, is so grave that all deserve to be punished by burning eternally in hell-fire.[21] Even a newborn

---

[21] "Original sin is the result of a sin committed, in actual historical fact, by an individual man named Adam, and it is a quality native to all of us, only because it has been handed down by descent from him."—Papal encyclical *Humani generis*, 1950; translation by R. A. Knox.

In his "The Catechism Simply Explained" (London, 1954, p. 62),

infant, dying in the moment of its birth, deserves this eternal torment.[22]

If we base our thinking on Abraham's premise, then we find ourselves asking how a person can be held responsible for any deed committed outside the jurisdiction of his will. Pelagius raised this question as early as the fifth century and was refuted by Augustine in his *De peccatorum meritis et remissione et de baptismo parrulorum.* He then called attention to the statement in Augustine's *De vera religione* that "sin is a voluntary evil to such an extent that where there is no will there is no sin." In his *Retractionum,* written toward the end of his life, Augustine responded by saying, in part: "Even what is called original sin in infants, although they do not yet enjoy the exercise of free will, is without absurdity called voluntary, since it followed upon the evil will of the first man and is in some way hereditary." This implies that the sin was an act of free will committed by an entity of which Adam and the infant, alike, are parts. It was not Adam's disobedience or the infant's, properly speaking. It was man's disobedience. If I were to be jailed for a murder would it not be absurd for me to plead that, since it was my right hand which did the deed, my left ought not to be punished along with it? If mankind is one person, then why is it not just as absurd to make moral distinctions among the particles of which that person is composed?

Jeremy Bentham tells us that "nature has placed mankind under the governance of two sovereign masters, *pain* and *pleasure.*"[23] But if we were asked where, precisely, the pain and pleasure were felt, we should have to answer that each

---

Canon Cafferata tells us that "the fire of hell is real fire of some kind," and the pain it causes is a "pain of sense."

[22] For discussion of a general falling away of belief in this doctrine, in modern times, see One, 26.

[23] The opening sentence of *An Introduction to the Principles of Morals and Legislation,* Chap. I.

physical person felt them separately. There could be no feelings of pleasure or pain felt by mankind but not felt by the individuals who composed it.

In a sense I, too, a physical person, am a collective noun like the state. My body is composed of cells organized in a single system. But if a needle pricks me what is it that feels pain? Do the cells directly in contact with the needle have an independent consciousness of pain in themselves? There is no reason to think that they do. The consciousness of pain belongs, rather, to the entity which I call "I," and my consciousness of the location of the pain is not the same as a local consciousness of the pain.

I conclude (1) that mankind, of which I am one cell, does not itself feel pleasure or pain; and (2) that the cells out of which I am composed do not feel pleasure or pain. These sensations are experienced only by a physical or individual person, not by any larger whole of which he is a component, nor yet by any of his own component parts. Sentience is what distinguishes individual persons from everything else and makes it impossible to deny their existence—as Paley denied the real existence of communities.

There is a philosophical limit, then, to which the status of the individual can be reduced. Paley may have been right or wrong in denying the real existence of communities. But it would be clearly wrong to deny the discrete existence of individual persons by equating them with the cells of an animal body.

The philosophical limit to which the status of the individual can be reduced constitutes, as well, a limit to which the status of the corporate person, composed of individuals, can be elevated. The integrity of the whole is limited by the independence of its parts.

SECTION 15

1. *"In repeated statements, Wilson made it clear that peace could not be made with the Kaiser and his government...."*

In a communication to the Pope of August 27, 1917, after saying that "the object of this war is to deliver the free peoples of the world from the menace and the actual power of a vast military establishment controlled by an irresponsible government," Wilson wrote: "This power is not the German people. It is the ruthless master of the German people. It is no business of ours how that great people came under its control or submitted with temporary zest to the domination of its purpose; but it is our business to see to it that the history of the rest of the world is no longer left to its handling."

With an explicit logic, an intellectual consistency of conscious thought such as one rarely finds in international politics, Wilson deliberately pressed for the prerequisites of the peace he had in mind. When, in October 1918, the rulers of Germany and the ruled, alike, were ready to end the war, he responded by a note in which he said: ". . . the President deems it his duty to say, without any attempt to soften what may seem harsh words, that the nations of the world do not and cannot trust the word of those who have hitherto been the masters of German policy, and to point out once more that in concluding peace and attempting to undo the infinite injuries and injustices of this war the Government of the United States cannot deal with any but veritable representatives of the German people who have been assured of a genuine constitutional standing as the real rulers of Germany. If it must deal with the military masters and the monarchical aristocrats of Germany now, or if it is likely to have to deal with them later in regard to the international obligations of the German Empire, it must demand, not peace negotiations, but surrender."

Fortune is not ordinarily indulgent to even the best-made plans of governments, but all now went according to heart's desire. An attempt by the Kaiser's régime to convert itself into a parliamentary government with a view to meeting Wilson's conditions was overtaken by a popular revolution which swept that régime away altogether, propelling the Kaiser into foreign exile, and established the representative government of the new Weimar Republic in its place. Suddenly there was no longer any enemy, according to Wilson's identification of the enemy, and it remained only to embrace the liberated German people.

If Wilson's reasoning was valid, there was no more reason to identify the Weimar régime with the misdeeds of the Kaiser than to identify Louis XVIII with the misdeeds of Napoleon. Germans, French, English, and Americans should now have been able to sit around the conference-table as friends and equals, having no quarrel with each other. Then peace might have been made on the terms set forth by Wilson when he said, "only a peace between equals can last."

Wilson's was a complicated mind. He was a political theorist and also a political leader. In choosing the line that he took in these quotations I suppose that he was not unmindful of the strategic advantages that would follow if a wedge could be driven between the German people and the German government. This still, however, would provide no reason to doubt his sincerity or the relevance of the line he took to the possibility of concluding a peace, once the war had been won.

It should be noted how neither Abraham nor David nor Wilson could quite bring himself to carry Paley's logic to its full length. Abraham found it prudent not to suggest sparing Sodom for the sake of less than ten righteous individuals, and there seems to have been no thought of destroying only the sinners in Sodom (perhaps, in the state of the destructive arts at that time, this would have presented insuperable technical difficulties). David, asking Yahweh not to punish the people of Jerusalem for a sin that he alone committed, does not suggest that the punishment fall only on him, but that it fall only on him and his father's house. Wilson, in the passages I have quoted, used a rhetoric in which the German people were implicitly presented as a corporate person capable of willing or not willing certain things.

2. *"No peace was made with the accredited representatives of the German people in 1919—if the definition of a peace is a genuine agreement to restore amicable relations on a basis of equality."*

In a volume entitled *Termination of War and Treaties of Peace*, published in London in 1916 (two years before the end of the war and three years before the conclusion of the Versailles settlement), Mr. Coleman Phillipson, defining a peace treaty in technical legal terms, wrote: "Where terms are dictated throughout to the utterly vanquished belligerent at the absolute discretion of the victor, the transaction cannot, strictly speaking, be designated a treaty: it is a unilateral imposition of demands. Every treaty of peace proper must have a bilateral character; it must involve reciprocal concessions, however unequal they may be. Even in earlier ages, when the *ius victoriae* was recognized and was in certain respects more cruel than the *ius belli*, we find such restrictions placed on the victorious combatant as to make his dealings with the defeated State a compromise. The object of the treaty of peace is not merely to put a stop to the war, but also to prevent its renewal; and this latter purpose is accomplished by means of a bargain settling each side's claims and pretensions."

Mr. Phillipson then went on to quote the eighteenth-century authority, Vattel, as follows: ". . . since it would be dreadful to perpetuate the war, or to pursue it to the utter ruin of one of the parties, and since, however just the cause in which we are engaged, we must at length turn our thoughts towards the restoration of peace, and ought to direct all our measures to the attainment of that salutary object, no other expedient remains than that of coming to a compromise respecting all claims and grievances on both sides, and putting an end to all disputes by a convention as fair and equitable as circumstances will admit of. In such conventions no decision is pronounced on the original cause of the war, or on those controversies to which the various acts of hostility might give rise; nor is either of the parties condemned as unjust. . . ."[24]

SECTION 16

The victors of 1814 and 1815, living in an age of such rapid transition, had every reason to be confused in their ideas of propriety. It was not only that, in the world to which they had been brought up, "the people" ought to be politically inert and obedient, the concepts of guilty states, of states that might properly be judged and punished, did not really belong to such a world. No matter how completely France under Louis XIV had been defeated, for example, the victors would hardly have thought either of punishing France or of punishing Louis personally, whether by cutting off his head or by deposing him. They would still have thought of re-establishing a European equilibrium in which France would have to bear its part; and Louis would have been expected to continue on the throne as the legitimate ruler of France by divine right, whether he was a scoundrel or not.

The case of Napoleon was less clear. He was essentially a usurper in the ranks of the European nobility; but Emperor Alexander of all the Russias had embraced him at Tilsit in 1807, and the Hapsburg emperor, Francis I, had given his daughter Marie Louise to be his empress. Napoleon had re-established order and control in France after the chaos of

[24] Pages 165-166.

the Revolution, and this was a respectable achievement in the eyes of the victors. There was serious thought, then, of leaving him on the French throne.

But his claim could not stand, in terms of legitimacy, against that of the head of the House of Bourbon who, at the initiative of Talleyrand, was now brought back from his exile in England and established on the throne of France as King Louis XVIII, by the grace of God. France, under the restored and legitimate rule of the Bourbons, was welcomed back into the family of nations. The son-in-law of the Hapsburg emperor, removed from the throne he had usurped, was given the island of Elba as a kingdom of his own in which he could continue to enjoy the rank of a European monarch.

By our twentieth-century standards this was dealing gently both with France and with Napoleon. When Napoleon, however, again showed his character as a usurping and aggressive adventurer by returning to France and taking its throne away from Louis XVIII, when he again mobilized the French people for the conquest of Europe, and when he had again to be defeated in battle, then the victors dealt with him somewhat less gently. They carried him off to captivity on the South Atlantic island of St. Helena, where he was an honored prisoner but no longer a monarch.

Certain onerous requirements to which France would otherwise have been compelled to submit were waived in the First Peace of Paris (1814) "now that, replaced under the paternal Government of her Kings, she offers the assurance of security and stability to Europe." After Napoleon returned from Elba the Allies "proclaimed that they were attacking not France but the Emperor; peace, then, might be secured by his abdication." They also signed a declaration "by which they bound themselves to aid Louis XVIII with all their strength."[25]

The Second Peace of Paris, made after Napoleon's tempo-

[25] *Cambridge Modern History*, Vol. I, Chap. XX.

rary return from Elba had upset the First, contained a few severities which the First did not have; but it still did not alter the fact that France, under the restored Bourbon monarchy, quickly took her full and honorable place in the concert of the great powers which swayed the destinies of Europe and made itself responsible for keeping the peace.

SECTION 17

1. "... *all the victors, as children of post-revolutionary times, attributed the actions of the state to the will of the people (in the case of the Western allies) or (in the case of the Soviet Union) to that of the enemies of the people.*"

The statements quoted from President Roosevelt represent the liberal democratic concept of "the people" as the total population of the state. But the Jacobin concept separates the species on class rather than national lines. We should have reason to be surprised if the rulers of the Soviet Union were ever to denounce "the people" rather than "the enemies of the people" anywhere.

In fact, one finds that Stalin did not make at all the same identification of the enemy in World War II as was made by the American and British members of the coalition against the Axis. He did not denounce the German or Italian "peoples," the German or Italian "nations," or "Germany" or "Italy." The following quotation shows how the enemy was identified in his eyes and suggests the unlikelihood that the Russians would find themselves in agreement with the Western democracies on postwar settlements with wartime enemies so differently identified. Addressing the Moscow Soviet on November 6, 1942, he said:

"In an interview with the Turkish General Erkilet, published in the Turkish newspaper *Cumhuriet*, that cannibal Hitler said: 'We shall destroy Russia so that she will never be able to rise again.' That would appear clear, although

163

rather silly. It is not our aim to destroy Germany, for it is impossible to destroy Germany, just as it is impossible to destroy Russia. But the Hitlerite state can and should be destroyed. And our first task in fact is to destroy the Hitlerite state and its inspirers.

"In the same interview with the same general, that cannibal Hitler went on to say: 'We shall continue the war until Russia ceases to have an organized military force.' That would appear clear although illiterate. It is not our aim to destroy all organized military force in Germany, for every literate person will understand that that is not only impossible in regard to Germany, as it is in regard to Russia, but also inadvisable from the point of view of the victor. But Hitler's army can and should be destroyed.

"Our second task, in fact, is to destroy Hitler's army and its leaders."

In this Jacobin view, all that was needed for the establishment of peace was the purging of "the enemies of the people" in the Axis countries and the other countries of East Europe associated with them. Once that was done, once the power of the state in each of those countries had been put into the hands of "the people," peace would be automatic.

2. *"In the Second World War the Western allies conducted their military operations and planned the post-war settlements on the premise that the world was divided between 'peace-loving' and 'aggressor' peoples."* All of us have the habit from earliest childhood of dividing mankind into two natural categories that stand opposed to each other. We identify ourselves with the one, which is human and loveable, while making the other the object of our fear and hatred. In our common thinking the essence of life is the combat between the two. It is represented in our tales for children and in our dramatic literature generally. That literature often has meaning for the reader to the extent that he is able

to identify himself with its heroes and to enjoy the sensations of horror and indignation inspired by its villains.

This concept of the two species, *We* and *They*, is generally carried over into the realm of history, into that long record of association and conflict among corporate persons. The American school-child, learning the history of the American Revolution, thinks of it as a conflict between the virtuous and the wicked. Reading the Bible stories, he finds the sufferings of Canaanites at the hands of Joshua and his hosts a source of gratification because, so far from identifying them as his own kind, he thinks of them as *They*, the representatives of an alien and evil species. For the same reason, he feels no horror at the destruction of Sodom.

This concept of species tends to dominate international relations in every age. "Therefore when Greeks and barbarians fight together," said Socrates, "we shall describe them as natural enemies, warring against one another; and to this kind of hostility we shall give the name of *war*: but when Greeks are on this sort of footing with Greeks, we shall say that they are natural friends, but that in the case supposed Greece is in a morbid state of civil conflict; and to this kind of hostility we shall give the name of *sedition*."[26] Many of us apply essentially the same distinction to cases of dissension between Communist governments, like the public quarrels that have taken place between the Soviet and Chinese governments, saying that they are "family quarrels" rather than quarrels between natural enemies. This is because we identify them as belonging to one species, opposed to the other species which is our own.

It was in terms of the two species that Christendom looked upon Islam and Islam upon Christendom at one time. In these terms the Communists have looked upon "the capitalist

[26] Plato, *The Republic*, translation by Davies and Vaughan, London, 1935, Book V, p. 182.

165

imperialists," and the nations on both sides of the Atlantic have looked upon the Communists.

This generally unpondered distinction, as it exists in our minds, is based on differences which are assumed to be native to the respective species, as poisoning is native to rattlesnakes. That is why it seems proper to kill all the people of Sodom without asking which of them have engaged in sinful acts; that is why Hitler felt justified in practicing genocide against the Jews; and that is why the Western democracies had so little compunction about dropping atomic bombs on the Japanese.

Both Judaism and Christianity have taught that one should cherish one's own kind. In the case of the most ancient Jews one's own kind meant one's own nation. The sixth of the ten commandments handed to Moses on Sinai, "You shall not kill," did not apply outside that nation. Just as it did not mean, you shall not step on a bug or slap a mosquito, so it did not forbid the children of Yahweh to kill the children of Chemosh, his rival. In the case of later Jews and of Christians, one's kind has generally had a larger meaning, but that meaning has still been less than universal. It has commonly excluded infidels, for example, or those conceived to be children of the devil. But even if we make the term synonymous with "all mankind" we may still have to face the question of how to define "all mankind."

In scientific terms man, today, is thought to constitute one species: the species *sapiens* of the genus *Homo*. Our problem is simplified by the fact that, in terms of these categories, all the other species of *Homo*, such as *H. soloensis*, have become extinct. If *H. soloensis* still walked the earth, then the question would surely arise whether he was our fellow man, the fellow man of *H. sapiens*; whether he was included in the brotherhood of man under the fatherhood of God.

If it is true that living men, today, are all representatives of one remaining species, then the scientific or theological

166

definition of man poses no practical problem. No one ventures to say that the Hottentot, much as he differs in physiognomy from the European (who everyone agrees is a man), is not a man. But there may have been more than one species when Christ preached, and even within living memory today.

The most primitive men known in modern times have been the Tasmanians, of which pure-blooded specimens still existed in the present century.[27] Some anthropologists have been disposed to regard them as belonging to a different species from ours, a *Homo tasmanianus*. The Christian European settlers of Australia who crossed the narrow waters to the island of Tasmania and there discovered the Tasmanians were neither scientists nor theologians. They and the Tasmanians seem, in an instinctive way, not to have regarded each other as fellow men. The Tasmanians were primitive specimens of humanity (if that is the right term for them) representing the level of development of prehistoric cave-dwellers, perhaps of the Crô-Magnon men. It might have been almost as hard for the Christians to establish communication and a mutual sense of community with them as with wild animals—or with *other* wild animals. What actually happened was that the Tasmanians set fire to the barns of the Christians and the Christians went out on Tasmanian-shoots as the New England settlers had gone on turkey-shoots.

These Christians were a rough lot, but we need not think of them as utterly devoid of Christian piety. The householder who hunted Tasmanians in his leisure time to clear the land for settlement may have prayed and gone to church regularly. He may have cherished his wife and children. He may

---

[27] *The Australian Encyclopaedia*, Sydney, 1958, Vol. I, pp. 104-6, reports that, "although both sexes usually went naked, individuals occasionally wore a kangaroo-skin hung over one shoulder." Referring to their language, it says: "It is doubtful whether numerals reached beyond two. There was no settled word order and instead of number, mood, and tense, gesticulations and signs were used to express shades of meaning." The white settlers, says the *Encyclopaedia*, "regarded the natives as subhuman and treated them accordingly."

have been kindly, helping his neighbor in affliction. He may have loved his fellow men. But he did not think of the Tasmanians as his fellow men.

Taking account of all the individuals who have ever lived, including those intermediate between modern men and the most primitive forms of early life, no biologist could find boundaries for "mankind"—except arbitrarily as a matter of linguistic convenience. In its evolution the branches of organic life have diverged continuously, rather than by the successive steps which our nominal categories of genus and species imply.[28] This poses a problem if one thinks of man as a species distinguished by the possession of a soul. Did *Homo soloensis* have a soul? If he did, did the species of the genus *Australopithecus* have souls? One may speculate that the ancestors of modern men were endowed with souls at a particular instant in their evolution, or alternatively that an element of soul was implicit in life from the beginning.

The question is whether there is more than one humankind. It is evident that the stock of *Homo sapiens* has in its evolution branched and rebranched. We see the consequences in the branch-ends that exist today. The branch-ends represented by the various races differ in physical characteristics, and so we must suppose that they differ in psychic characteristics as well (especially if we accept the modern scientific view which makes no sharp separation between the physical and the psychological). It is plausible that, just as one branch is shorter in body-height than another, or one branch shows more vitality than another, so one branch should be more aggressive than another. Although the terms might leave something to be desired in the way of scientific precision, the concept of "peace-loving" nations and "aggressor" nations might represent, however roughly, an anthropological reality. Perhaps Germany is an "aggressor" by racial inheritance, and France a "peace-loving" nation.

[28] See Two, 25, 2.

168

What we are trying to do here is to equate the concept of opposed species, as it governs the thinking and behavior of men in communities, with possible genetic differences among those communities. The minute we embark on this attempt, however, we are confronted with all the instances in which this concept has divided mankind on lines that do not correspond to its racial divisions. The concept is well exemplified in the repeated statements of those who spoke for the Atlantic allies in World War II that the world was divided between "peace-loving" and "aggressor" nations. When we ask which nations were conceived to belong to which species we are told that the United States, the United Kingdom, the Soviet Union, and China belonged to the "peace-loving" species, while Germany, Italy, and Japan belonged to the "aggressor" species. Here is a division that lends itself poorly to the racial distinction which is proposed.

If we look at the long record of human conflict, in which the concept of opposed species has played so dominant a part, we generally get the same negative result as in the case of the Second World War. Conflict between communities has rarely been on racial lines. Religious, political, and economic grounds of conflict appear to have been far commoner, at least in historic times. Consequently, those who represent the concept of opposed species have rarely been able to do more than to suggest in vague or unsupported ways that it has a genetic basis.

3. Morley Roberts's description of the German people as a corporate person engaged in a secret conspiracy against the world is the counterpart of the anti-semitic propaganda in Germany that described the Jews as a corporate person engaged in a secret conspiracy against the world. If the Germans or the Jews were thought of as existential realities, it would immediately be altogether implausible that tens of millions of them could actually conspire together in secret.

At the end of Two, 14, we noted that "the philosophical

limit to which the status of the individual can be reduced constitutes, as well, a limit to which the status of the corporate person, composed of individuals, can be elevated. The integrity of the whole is limited by the independence of its parts." Mr. Roberts, in the quotation under reference, has practiced a trick of rhetoric upon us: he has presented a metaphorical image in the guise of literal truth. Although men may be compared to the protoplasmic cells that compose an animal organism, they are not that in literal reality. For protoplasmic cells are not persons in their own right; they have no power to move by themselves; they have no will nor any capacity for sensation by themselves. When we talk about men as the cells of an animal body we are doing what we do when we talk about an "angry" sea. But when Mr. Roberts, by pretending that his metaphor is literal truth, makes an argument for genocide, it is as if he proposed to punish the sea for acting in anger. He is taking literally a figure of speech that has no literal standing.

4. *"In 1945 the theory of 'the people's' responsibility made peace impossible, even after the ruler had been removed from the scene."*

In the Second World War there was no such conscious and deliberate attempt to limit the identification of the enemy as Wilson, in the role of Abraham, had made during the First World War. But the Atlantic Charter (1941) implied that the enemy was "the Hitlerite government of Germany and other governments associated therewith. . . ." It set the allied goal as "the final destruction of the Nazi tyranny," and it promised at least a certain equality of economic opportunity to all states, "victor or vanquished," once the goal had been attained.

Even in the Atlantic Charter, however, the concept that the nations of the world are naturally divided into two species has its expression. There is a reference to keeping "nations which threaten, or may threaten, aggression" disarmed when the war is over. In the intellectual climate of the time there was no need to say how one might recognize such nations, since one already knew which they were.

In a radio address on Christmas Eve of 1943 the President read a lesson from history: "After the Armistice in 1918, we thought and hoped that the militaristic philosophy of Germany had been crushed; and being full of the milk of human kindness we spent the next fifteen years disarming, while the Germans whined so pathetically that the other nations permitted them—and even helped them—to rearm. For too many years we lived on pious hopes that aggressor and warlike nations would learn and understand and carry out the doctrine of purely voluntary peace. The well-intentioned but ill-fated experiments of former years did not work. It is my hope that we will not try them again. . . . If the people of Germany and Japan are made to realize thoroughly that the world is not going to let them break out again, it is possible, and, I hope, probable, that they will abandon the philosophy of aggression."

SECTION 18

1. *"The abstraction is one's enemy; the existential reality is one's fellow man."*

A Japanese lady, who had been in a small Japanese town when the first American occupation troops came in, told me of an incident that illustrates the theme of this chapter.

The Japanese people, having come to believe that the Americans were ravening monsters, awaited their coming in terror. A group of women were standing in the market-square when a little old woman, half laughing and half crying, came running to them. She had, she told them, just seen her first American. Walking along a certain street, she had seen approaching her a tall figure in an American soldier's uniform. Her impulse had been to run away. Thinking, however, of her honor as a Japanese she had stood her ground, although in terrible fear.

Then an astonishing thing happened. The American took off his cap, and his hair was golden. He smiled directly down at her, and his eyes were blue. It was such a sunny smile, and so unexpected, that suddenly she had an outlandish thought. Suddenly, she told her friends, she wanted to have a son like that.

2. A moral dilemma involved in the paradox of the two worlds may be illustrated by imagining what might happen if, at the Nüremberg Trials after World War II, the entity which the Allied leaders had held primarily responsible for the War, the German people, had been brought up for trial. We shall put ourselves in the seats of the judges, and we shall suppose the worst of the accused—i.e., that Hitler represented the well-nigh universal consensus of the German people, who had in overwhelming preponderance supported his policies.

What is the specific charge, now, against the German nation?

It is charged with waging aggressive war, an act that the Nüremberg Military Tribunal (which actually did sit in judgment in 1945-1946) declared to be the "supreme international crime." In view of all the evidence, we, the judges, could hardly avoid a finding of guilty. And we have ample precedent for declaring a community, as such, guilty. That precedent antedates Yahweh's judgment on Sodom and is represented as late as 1919 by Article 231 of the Versailles Treaty, which embodied a finding that "Germany" (independently of her governing régime) was responsible for the First World War. In fact, Germany comes before us as a second offender, and we may suppose that the verdict we reach is, once more, guilty.

Having determined the fact of guilt, what do we, the judges, do about it? Presumably the mission of judges is to realize justice. Justice is done when its subjects are given their due: due punishment for the wrongdoer, due recompense for his victim. Germany, a corporate person, has committed what is officially recognized to be the "supreme" crime. What is the due of such a person? Is it not what the criminal law of most civilized countries recognizes as the "supreme" penalty, the sentence of death? As a matter of pure justice, then, excluding all other considerations, whether of practicality or mercy, we would surely be correct in imposing on Germany the same sentence that Yahweh imposed on Sodom.

So far we have been addressing ourselves to the object of justice only in its abstract aspect. At this point, however, it becomes hard for persons as advanced in civilization as we are to keep the other aspect from forcing itself upon our consciousness. We are likely to find that the Abraham in us begins to contend, at this point, with the Yahweh. Though the sentence is to be passed on an abstraction, we see that it will be executed on concrete individual persons, on the flesh-and-blood of men, women, and children. The question which Abraham posed for Yahweh, and which at least gave Yahweh pause, is now posed for us. Even Mr. Morley Roberts—that civilized Englishman who had advocated death by genocide for the German nation—might wish to consider, at this point, a proposition to the effect, let us say, that infants under the age of two be exempted. Or if, regarding them as an abstract class, he remained unmoved, then the question posed with respect to a particular infant brought into court in its mother's arms, obviously unaware either of wrongdoing or of its peril, might finally break his resolution even as the resolution of Coriolanus had been broken by the appeal of his mother made in her own person. In like fashion, the bombardier who dropped an atom-bomb on a city many thousands of feet below him could not, I suppose, have taken his knife to cut the throat of even one of the babies that perished in the consequent blast.

At this point, then, the abstract reality has given way before the concrete, which has at last forced its way into the courtroom. We, the judges, see before us a succession of individual persons. These persons, when we see them close up, are unmistakably like us, and perhaps not altogether like the abstract images we had had in mind. They manifestly belong to humanity, not to some alien and demonic species as, in other circumstances, we might have imagined.

The German people, now, pass before us as individuals. Perhaps the first to come is a six-month-old infant. It seems a bit hard to point our finger at this component of the people and accuse him of complicity in Hitler's crimes. He has an alibi, since he was not on this mundane scene when the crimes were committed. We could hold him responsible on the principle that the sins of the fathers must be visited on the children, the principle exemplified in the doctrine of original sin. But this principle is more plausible when we are dealing with the abstract reality than when we are dealing with a particular infant who smiles and cries just like one of our own.

The second to be brought before us is an old peasant woman from the Bavarian Alps whose crotchets make it hard to suppress one's smiles. Asked whether she was in favor of extirpating the Jews, she says that indeed she was! Here, then, is self-confessed guilt. But someone asks her if she has ever seen a Jew or knows what one is like. She clicks her tongue with impatience at the question. What if she hasn't actually seen a Jew? Everyone knows what they are like. What *are* they like? the court asks. She then presents the image of the Jew as a demonic spirit disguised in human flesh, working secretly as an agent of Satan to bring about the downfall of God's Creation. Jews slew Abel; they crucified Christ. She says that they can be identified by their

174

cloven hooves, if you can get their shoes off (which is not easy). This raises the question whether she really had any clear notion of what she was supporting when she supported the policy of getting rid of Germany's Jews. Her case is the same on the other relevant issues. She was in favor of the campaign against Poland because, as Hitler declared, the Poles were committing intolerable atrocities against German women. (No, of course she was not in Poland and did not see these things with her own eyes!) It was to save the German women that the gallant German soldiers marched into Poland. Proper men have the sacred duty of defending the honor of their womenfolk.[29]

Not many cases are quite as extreme as this. On the other hand, the informed students of international relations among the German people are equally few. What most of the individuals know is what the *de facto* authorities tell them. They lack the basis for independent individual judgments.

The next to be brought in after the old woman is the fat bandmaster of a village band in Saxony who was also the village barber. This man joined the Nazi Party and did its bidding. Why? He can't exactly say, not having the gifts of introspection and self-expression, but a number of reasons transpire in the course of the inquest. For one thing, every-

---

[29] This old woman illustrates the role that ignorance plays in easing the problem of reconciling abstract with concrete reality. As one of the people who bear the responsibility of power (under the theory on which she is here brought to trial, the theory embodied in the Preamble of the Charter of the United Nations), she is called upon to have responsible views on the Jewish people and on events in Poland. Having no experience of the concrete reality in either case, her views can be based only on what has been presented to her in the guise of an abstract reality. Since she cannot feel the need to reconcile the abstraction with experience that she has never had, it holds the field by itself, undisputed.

The ignorant live in a world of untested abstractions. What the reader should note, however, is that in this the old peasant woman does not differ so widely from a university professor as, at first thought, one might suppose. How many American professors with opinions about international relations know the concrete reality of China, or of Pakistan? They, too, depend on conceptions of abstract reality largely untested by experience of concrete reality.

body joined. Like people everywhere, he conformed auto-matically to his environment. He was not, after all, a political philosopher equipped to think for himself. (He keeps repeat-ing that he is not a learned man like his judges, bowing each time he says it.) One cannot doubt that in Britain he would have been for democracy, in Russia for Communism. His mistake was to be in Germany. Hitler was the Führer, and it was treason not to follow the Führer.

So they pass by, "the German people" in their concrete reality, each one an essentially unique case. But there are certain broad categories (associations by likeness) to be roughly distinguished. There are men and women who were opposed in their hearts to Hitler and the Nazis, though most of these were unwilling to risk making martyrs of them-selves by engaging in active opposition. (What is, perhaps, more surprising is that some did.) There are other cases in which a man, putting the survival of his wife and children above other considerations, obeyed the Nazis in order to keep his job or his business. There are some cases of violent and fanatical young men who became ardent followers of Hitler, believing (with all the wisdom of adolescence) that he would rid the country, at last, of its ignoble, unheroic, decadent elements, that he would at last break the sordid bonds of frustration which had fettered Germany's natural greatness. Finally, there are defendants, not a few, who ap-pear essentially evil, educated men with good minds who deliberately conspired against their fellow men in the quest of personal power or wealth, or in the satisfaction of per-verted lusts. I repeat that these would not be few.

Any judge who came to know the German people in this fashion, one by one, would surely find abhorrent evils in them, evils that sickened or outraged him. But the reason for his sickness and outrage might be rather complex, per-haps not involving only what he discovered to exist in persons other than himself. In fact, the better he knew himself, the

godlike. When he comes to the hut of his swineherd, Eumaeus, after ten years of adventures that have aged him, he wears the aspect of a broken old man; but when he stands, at last, revealed to the son from whom he has been so long separated, he is transfigured by Athena's grace: relieved of his human infirmities, he stands erect before Telemachus, now, like a god.

Surely this represents common experience—the experience of feeling oneself a lame sort of creature, and the occasional contrasting experience of feeling oneself transfigured by some inward grace that, in our own terminology, we have associated with the *Logos*.

The dual nature of Jesus, as son of man and son of God, represents the same experience. In Matthew 17:1-2, we read how "Jesus took with him Peter and James and John his brother, and led them up a high mountain apart. And he was transfigured before them, and his face shone like the sun, and his garments became white as light."

2. *"To show what life really is, Joyce replaces Homer's Ulysses with the ungodlike Mr. Leopold Bloom, whose adventures, because they are unheroic, correspond to daily experience as those of Homer's Ulysses do not."*

Take, as an example, the following passage in which Bloom muses to himself on how his son (the counterpart of Telemachus) was conceived: "Must have been that morning in Raymond terrace she was at the window, watching the two dogs at it by the wall of the cease to do evil. And the sergeant grinning up. She had that cream gown on with the rip she never stitched. Give us a touch, Poldy. God, I'm dying for it. How life begins."[37]

3. *"Here ... the issue is drawn between the dual philosophy and those opposed philosophies—nihilism, positivism, materialism, nominalism—that deny the reality of anything except what is physically manifest."*

[37] Hamburg, 1932, p. 92.

185

Each of these labels applies to a variety of philosophical doctrines. I use them here in reference to those doctrines that fit the following limited definitions.

Nihilism: *"Doctrine d'après laquelle rien n'existe (d'absolu)* [Doctrine according to which nothing has an absolute existence]"; or *"Doctrine d'après laquelle il n'y a point de vérité morale, pas de hiérarchie des valeurs* [Doctrine according to which there is no moral truth, no hierarchy of values]."[38]

Positivism: The various doctrines that attribute reality to nothing that is not verifiable by scientific observation and proof.

Materialism: *"Doctrine d'après laquelle il n'existe d'autre substance que la matière, à laquelle on attribue des propriétés variables suivant les diverses formes de matérialisme, mais qui a pour caractère commun d'être conçue comme un ensemble d'objets individuels, représentables, figurés, mobiles, occupant chacun une région déterminée de l'espace* [Doctrine according to which no substance exists other than matter, to which various properties are attributed, according to the various forms of materialism, but which have as a common characteristic that of being conceived as a collection of individual objects, susceptible of being represented, of being pictured, of moving, each occupying a set space]."[39] "This view comprises . . . the more specific thesis that human beings and other living creatures are not dual beings composed of a material body and an immaterial soul, but are fundamentally bodily in nature."[40]

Nominalism: This is the doctrine that generalizing concepts or abstractions ("universals") are words, not realities in themselves. I have held here that the generalizing con-

[38] André Lalande (ed.), *Vocabulaire Technique et Critique de la Philosophie*, Paris, 1960, p. 681.

[39] *Ibid.*, p. 591.

[40] J. O. Urmson (ed.), *The Concise Encyclopaedia of Western Philosophy and Philosophers*, London, 1960, pp. 253-254.

186

cepts or abstractions in the human mind are words, not realities in themselves; but I have not accepted the further implication that they are necessarily so, or that only physical objects are real, and I have also held that the concepts in the human mind may approximate more or less closely that primary and non-physical reality which I have called the *Logos*.

I have not listed "existentialism" among the philosophies that stand opposed to the dual philosophy because, historically, it is hardly more than a disposition, which I share, to attach special value to the existential world (as Paley did), disciplining one's thinking by constant reference to it. It sometimes implies, but does not necessarily imply, that there is nothing outside of existential reality.

I have also refrained from listing the belief that is described by the term "cultural relativism" because it is hardly a rounded philosophy in itself. It is, however, as conspicuous in our present world as those philosophies I have mentioned. What it amounts to is the view that all values, including moral values, are functions of the particular cultural setting in which they occur, and that they are merely this. Nothing is good or bad, better or worse, except as a matter of the mores of a particular society.

The role of cultural conditioning seems to me undeniable. My dissent comes only at the point where I am told that no values have a greater basis of validity.

4. Suppose we accept the nihilistic premise that there are no absolute values, that the values we regard as absolute are merely relative to the conceptual worlds, themselves illusions, in which we have been brought up.

This was the message of Sigmund Freud, whose thought responded to what a disciple has called his "rude, persistent demand for the bodily origin of spiritual things."[41] To him a work of art, far from being a product of divine inspiration,

---

[41] Norman O. Brown, *Life against Death: The Psychoanalytical Meaning of History*, London, 1959, p. 25.

was no more than a sublimated expression of the artist's frustrated libido, symptomatic of an animal impulse that does not distinguish man from the beasts. What it represents is known to every dog in the streets.

Let us accept this and apply it to a sample of experience.

The High Mass in B-minor, by Johann Sebastian Bach, is a kind of communication, as any piece of music is a kind of communication.

What does it communicate?

Seated in the church where it is being performed, and listening to it with an innocent ear, it seems to me to communicate the vision of a world of perfect order and harmony that contrasts with the disorder and the disharmony of this existential world. But this, I admit, is illusion.

I leave the church, now, and emerge into a land where the juke-box rules. Over a loud-speaker I hear a woman testifying to the method by which she keeps her underarms dry.

I pass on down the street, coming to where a ragged infant in the gutter, egged on to it by some older boys, is smearing its face with filth. . . .

I pass on to where a candidate for political office is haranguing a group of idlers. His body has spread with easy living and corruption in the back rooms until his belly stretches his pants. Putting his thumbs under his armpits and looking around at the audience he says: "I'm an American. And what I'm for is America. If there's anyone here who's not a good American I want to know it. I want him to step out in front of this here crowd, and stand here under this blessed flag of ours, and say so. . . ."

I pass on to where some boys have knocked down an old man. One of them is rifling his pockets, while another in occasional spasms of violence kicks his body. The old man keeps trying to lift his head, and inarticulate sounds of animal anguish come from it. . . .

It is late night when I go down a flight of stairs to where the

188

subway-trains run under the city. On the platform, as a train roars in, a child (he cannot be over six years old) is tugging at the hand of his drunken father, trying to get him onto the train. The father, a tall workman in dirty unbuttoned clothes, staggers back and forth across the platform, muttering to himself, sometimes croaking snatches of song. He is too strong for the child, who sobs and cries as he tries to get him onto the train. But the train closes its doors and moves on, gaining speed. The father, in a sudden gesture, flings the child from him. The child picks himself up and, sobbing still, comes back to take his father's hand and cling to it as if all safety and happiness were in it alone.

This sequence of experience, from the music of the Mass to the antics of the drunken father, displays a contrast that I cannot escape. It seems to me to be a contrast between higher and lower, between better and worse. I know, however, that the scale of values which forms the basis for this judgment has no standing in the universe. I know that, except with respect to my own conditioning, there is no higher and lower, no better and worse. The croaking of the drunkard stands at the same level as the Mass.

Bach, I know, was essentially as bestial as any dog in the streets, as bestial as the boys that assaulted the old man. He was moved to compose the Mass by his libido, by an animal drive which found its sublimated fulfillment in the composition—by the same impulse, perhaps, that caused the boy to kick the body of the old man. The vision that it communicates to me is to be explained in terms of such sublimation, in terms of the fictions on which we depend to make life tolerable. It is an escape from reality, from the reality represented by the child trying to bring his drunken father home. What the music communicates is the heroic illusion, the illusion which Freud and Joyce and other writers have now revealed for what it is.

Accepting, then, the fact that all human creation can be

explained in terms of our animal natures, am I to consider the quest for understanding completed at last?

But ahead of me, along the road of inquiry, I still see unanswered questions. For example: Why is it that a dog whose libidinous appetite is frustrated does not compose a B-minor Mass? Or: Why is it that all men whose libidinous appetites are frustrated do not produce works equivalent to the B-minor Mass? May not the sublimation of the libido find varying expressions that can be compared as higher and lower? Perhaps the drunken father got drunk because, suffering the same frustration but lacking some special quality which Bach had, he could not find the same kind of release. Is there not some difference of higher and lower, here, between the composition of the music and the drunken orgy?

But both, we may still say, found escape in illusion—Bach in the illusion of his vision, the father in the illusions that accompanied his drunkenness. Perhaps the only grounds for saying that Bach's sublimation was higher than the drunkard's are the relative grounds of social utility. These are not grounds for believing that the libido can have a higher or a lower expression in absolute terms.

Bach's vision has a quality of nobility that we may suppose to be lacking in the vision of the drunkard. But, since the vision is of a world that is not real, the nobility must be an illusion. I grant that it is.

See, however, what a verbal paradox this gets us into. A dream may be real or unreal in the sense that one does or does not have it. One can really dream something, or one can pretend that one dreamed something which one did not dream. An illusion is real as, at least, an illusion. It is a real illusion. Bach's vision is a real vision in the sense that he had it. And from the fact that he had it follows the fact that his mind or imagination had the capacity for it—a capacity which, perhaps, distinguishes him from the dog and the drunkard.

Descartes said: "I think, therefore I am." Might he not have said with equal point: "I think nobly, therefore I am noble"?

If the human mind dwells, on occasion, at an exalted level, then the reality of such a level, at which the mind is capable of dwelling, is established. Exaltation is real because the mind has experienced it, and the question of illusion is irrelevant. Noble illusions are noble.

The question of utility is also irrelevant. The experience of exaltation is sufficient in itself, it justifies itself, and it does not matter whether it happens to serve some useful ulterior purpose as well.

The reader will note that this logic still has no implication of an absolute scale of values against which to measure the levels of conception. I acknowledge that this is so and freely confess, now, that the criteria of higher and lower exist in my own mind, and that I cannot prove their existence elsewhere. For how can I prove the existence of anything outside my own mind? I cannot prove that day and night exist outside my own mind. Nevertheless, my experience leads me to identify these criteria with the universe in which I live. For me they are there as day and night are there; and I must let my life be governed by them as I let my life be governed by the alternations of the day and the night. I could reject them only as I could refuse to get out of bed in the morning because I did not know that the daylight existed objectively.[41a]

Just as our own apprehension of day and night leads us to order our lives accordingly, so our apprehension of the ideal world justifies us in assuming its status as a fact of nature.

SECTION 23

"A critic might hold that the test . . . is simply a practical

[41a] The problem here is the epistemological problem dealt with in Chapter II.

one, based on the difference between those who construct and those who destroy. ..."

The distinction between utilitarian criteria of judgment and criteria representing absolute value holds good, I suspect, only at a relatively superficial level, in terms of a relatively petty utility. Ultimately, it would be pointless to argue about whether harmony and wholeness are good in themselves or good in that they work well. If we ever get close enough to the Kingdom of Heaven to peer over the edge, no doubt we shall see that the question does not arise.

SECTION 24

". . . we do better to think of it, not as a particular and transient philosophical system, but as philosophy itself. It would follow that the formal systems which stand opposed to it (positivism, materialism, etc.) are to be classified as anti-philosophy."

I confess that this statement involves a certain play with the word "philosophy." In its most general sense, the word stands for a conception of being, and of the possibilities of knowledge, from which nothing is excluded *a priori.* But it has a variety of narrower meanings in common usage—for which I refer the reader to the articles on "Philosophe" and "Philosophie" in the *Vocabulaire Technique et Critique de la Philosophie* by André Lalande. Here he will find an observation by J. Lachelier from which I quote the following: *"La philosophie me paraît être essentiellement . . . la métaphysique; et la métaphysique est . . . la science des conditions a priori de l'existence et de la vérité, la science de la raison et de la rationalité universelles, la science de la pensée en elle-même et dans les choses. . . . —L'empirisme est-il une philosophie? Oui, en ce sens qu'il pose et ne peu pas ne pas poser la question de la rationalité universelle, mais comme il la résout négativement, il doit être appelé une philosophie négative, ou même une négation de la philoso-phie* [Philosophy seems to me to be, essentially, . . . meta-physics, and metaphysics is . . . the science of the *a priori* con-ditions of existence and truth, the science of reason and universal rationality, the science of thought in itself and in things. . . . Is empiricism a philosophy? Yes, in the sense that it poses and necessarily must pose the question of universal rationality; but as it resolves that question negatively, it must be called a negative philosophy, or even a negation of philosophy]."[42]

If the undertaking of philosophy is to define truth, then a doctrine that says there is no truth may not improperly be regarded as a negation of philosophy, therefore an anti-philosophy. If the undertaking of philosophy is to define ultimate values, then a doctrine that says there are no ultimate values may be regarded as an anti-philosophy. Such doc-trines may represent philosophy in the broadest definition of the term, but they represent anti-philosophy in the nar-rower definition that I am using at this point.

SECTION 25

1. *"Because the nominal ideas and the nominal things exist for us as names in the first instance, the logic implicit in their names tends to replace, in our minds, the logic im-plicit in their reality."*

An example, beside those given in this chapter, is that of "The Bulldogs" and "The Rangers" in One, 8.

2. *"Today the white European nation to which the name 'Turkey' is applied bears no resemblance, in its existential reality, to the Mongoloid nation called 'Turkey' that estab-lished itself at the eastern end of the Mediterranean ten centuries ago."*

The Turks were yellow-skinned Orientals, belonging to

[42] Paris, 1960, pp. 773-774.

that succession of nations on horseback which emerged from Central Asia to conquer far and wide over the Eurasian continent. The land in which they finally settled had been inhabited from the beginning of the historical record by white Europeans called Slavs. The Slavs were subjugated by the Mongol Turks, but in the course of the centuries the Mongol Turks were absorbed by the Slavs, with whom they intermarried, and at last disappeared. They left their name, however, on the Slavs who remained when they had disappeared.

The disjunction between name and reality is the commonest cause of confusion in our thinking, and consequently merits examination.

Botanists, in their list of North American plants, include three species of aster, to wit: *Aster macrophyllus, A. herveyi,* and *A. spectabilis*. When one tries to identify specimens of them in nature, however, one runs into trouble. Any individual plant, dissected and its parts examined under a microscope, may appear to be intermediate, in its diagnostic characteristics, between *macrophyllus* and *herveyi*, or between *herveyi* and *spectabilis*. Moreover, there is such a range of variation within what is called the one species *macrophyllus* that some botanists have been tempted to divide it into several species (viz., *A. pinguifolius, A. excelsior, A. velutinus, A. sejunctus, A. apricensis, A. ianthinus, A. violaris, A. multiformis,* and *A. nobilis*).

All this is bewildering to anyone who has not grasped the distinction between what is nominal and what is real. Species are nominal categories that do not exist in nature. (God, one might say, did not create species.) What exists in nature is a continuum, varying without any abrupt transition through what are called *macrophyllus, herveyi,* and *spectabilis*.

Likewise, there is an unbroken continuum in nature between the ruby-throated hummingbird and the American bald eagle. In this case, it is hidden from us by the fact that intermediate forms have become extinct; but if one could lay out in a graded row the skins of all the individual birds that had ever lived, they would show a continuous gradation from the one extreme to the other.

Orders, families, genera, species—these are nominal categories only. They are not real.

Some years ago, persons all over the world were distressed by the death, on Martha's Vineyard, of the last "heath hen" in the world, and the consequent extinction of its kind. But "heath hen" was merely a name given to the Eastern American variety of what, in the West, was called "prairie chicken." If the usual practice had been followed, it too would have been called "prairie chicken" (perhaps the absence of prairies in the East was the reason for giving it a different name), in which case no one would have considered that it had become extinct and the distress of conservationists would, at least, have been lessened.

The ivory-billed woodpecker of the United States (*Campephilus principalis*) is either extinct or about to be extinct today. A woodpecker on the island of Cuba, however, resembles it so closely that taxonomists may decide, one of these days, that it is the same species, to be identified by the same name. If that happens, then the ivory-billed woodpecker, having been extinct, will be so no longer.

In the middle of the last century something called the "T'ai P'ing" movement almost succeeded in capturing China. It identified itself as Christianity, and Christian missionaries who accepted this nominal identification as real looked forward breathlessly to the prospective Christianization of half of Asia. But it was so outlandish in its doctrine that other Christian missionaries were moved to regard it as either heretical Christianity or not Christianity at all (depending on whether heretical Christianity is Christianity, a question in nominal logic rather than in reality). So the conflict between nominal and real caused pellmell intellectual confusion among all concerned.

The continuum of reality extends in time as well as space; but, while things change in time, their names do not. A number of years ago, the alumni of a school I had gone to as a boy held a meeting to discuss the possibility of saving it from being discontinued. I shared the general eagerness to save it until, looking into the matter, I concluded that it was the same school I had attended only in name. As I now saw the situation, the school I had attended had long ago vanished, but this fact had been hidden from me and my fellow alumni by the persistence of the nominal situation. We had given our allegiance to a name that now stood for something different from what it had stood for when we had given it our allegiance.[43]

If this can be true of a school, which is given a categorical character by formal organization, how much more true must it be of an ideology, a "body of belief" like "Communism."

A classic question in philosophy is whether, if one replaces the blade of a knife this year and its handle next year, it is still the same knife. We think of it as the same knife because the same word is applied to it—it is still, let us say, "my knife." Suppose, however, that the knife-blade is replaced by the blade of a screwdriver, and the knife-handle by the handle of a screwdriver. In that case it would not be the same "knife" but a "screwdriver" that had been made out of it. The question, which is how much a thing can change and still be the same thing, has no meaning in terms of the existential world. It has meaning only in terms of the nominal world in which our minds have their primary habitation. We answer it by either keeping or changing the old name.

It is not easy to grasp the notion that, in a view which transcended time and space, the ruby-throated hummingbird

[43] Cf. Two, 9, 5.

and the bald eagle would be one and the same, a single entity—indeed, that I and the amoeba would be one. The monism which this implies was expressed as follows by Spinoza in a letter to a correspondent:[44]

"If we consider quantity as it is in the imagination (which is the common and easy way) it will be found divisible, finite, made up of parts, and manifold. But if we consider Substance as it is in the understanding, and the thing is considered as it is in itself, which is exceedingly difficult, then, as I have at former times sufficiently shown you, it will be found infinite, indivisible, and single.

"Again, from the fact that we can assign bounds to duration and quantity at our pleasure (that is, when we conceive quantity abstractly apart from Substance, and separate duration in our thought from the manner of its derivation from eternal things) there arise Time and Measure; Time being conceived in order to determine duration, Measure in order to determine quantity, so that we may most conveniently represent them in imagination. Then from the fact that we separate the affections of Substance from Substance itself and reduce them to classes for the like convenience of our imagination, there arises Number, whereby we determine the same. Whereby it is plainly to be seen that measure, time, and number are nothing else than ways of thinking, or rather of imagining."

3. *"If Marx had returned to earth he might well have regarded what was still called 'Communism' as representing a rival set of ideas, opposed to what he had stood for himself."*

The picture of Karl Marx returning to earth to discover what has happened to "Communism" belongs to the essential theme of the Grand Inquisitor's story in Dostoievsky's *The Brothers Karamazov*. Here the point I have made in this chapter is carried to its logical and convincing conclusion.

---

[44] Letter to Dr. Lewis Meyer (Ep. xii), quoted in Sir Frederick Pollock, *Spinoza*, London, 1935, p. 73.

4. *"We attach ourselves to the immutable name, thereby escaping from the flux in which we might otherwise drown."*

As we have already observed,[45] we are all disposed to accept the features of our passing environment as normal and permanently established, as representing the purpose of God or nature, as representing the same propriety for us that the hive represents for the bees. The nation-state (or democracy, or the rule of the Hapsburgs) represents what God intended. We are like passengers in a moving train taking snapshots from the windows to show where we have at last arrived. Plato and Aristotle photograph the city-state, Aquinas and Dante photograph the universal empire, Hobbes photographs the despotic state, Locke photographs the Whig state, Hegel photographs the nation-state; and each presents his photograph as the model to be studied in place of the imperfect, elusive, and fleeting existential reality. Each seeks to stop the process of change by substituting an ideal nominal world for the existential world. Each, though he advocates improvements, is trying to stop the flow of time. Each is trying to conserve, which is why he may advocate those changes which, in fact, constitute repairs to the structure that is the object of conservation.[46]

But the train will not be arrested. Just as we expend our individual lives in a continuous progress toward death, so every feature of our society is obsolescent from its first appearance. "All passes, all changes. . . ." This is the most poignant theme of art and literature, which forever seek to immortalize what cannot last.

[45] Two, 9, *1.*

[46] This does not apply, or it applies only with qualifications, to revolutionary philosophers like Rousseau and Marx. But his native state of Geneva was the basis of Rousseau's model, and even Marx, who was an active revolutionary as Rousseau never thought of being, took the class-struggle of his time as the model for human society, until that day when it would resolve itself at last in an eschatological end equivalent to the Last Judgment and the coming of the Kingdom of Heaven on Earth.

But thy eternal summer shall not fade,
Nor lose possession of that fair thou ow'st,
Nor shall death brag thou wander'st in his shade,
When in eternal lines to time thou grow'st;
    So long as men can breathe, or eyes can see,
    So long lives this, and this gives life to thee.[47]

The nominal world endures as the real world does not. The portrait-painter's work is there, still, long ages after its sitter has mouldered into dust. The Greeks were not satisfied until at last they could express their vision in stone temples rather than wooden; and those temples remain today to speak for them, thousands of years after they have gone. In the nominal world Heraclitus still lives.

And now that thou art lying, my dear old Carian guest,
A handful of gray ashes, long, long ago at rest,
Still are thy pleasant voices, thy nightingales, awake;
For Death, he taketh all away, but them he cannot take.[48]

So long as men can hear, the voices continue to sound after the singers are dead. But, with the continuation of change, men may eventually lose the faculty of hearing what their forebears heard. Then, when ears become deaf, the voices fall silent at last.

It is no good for a Jean Bodin or a Bossuet, gazing upon the new foundations of divine right, to say: We have arrived. In a couple of centuries men will be forced to recognize that these foundations are becoming obsolete, that they no longer afford the sure support which Bodin and Bossuet found in them. Either they have to be remodeled (as the English were constantly doing) or, if clung to overlong, they will at last collapse in such chaos as that of the French Revolution. Then another nominal model becomes established, perhaps that of the nation-state, and political philosophers claim again that

---

[47] Shakespeare, *Sonnet XVIII.*   [48] W. J. Cory, *Heraclitus.*

199

we have arrived. The illusion of stability prevails because the nominal, which dominates our minds, remains unchanged even while the existential reality evolves. But again the passage of time brings increasing obsolescence. The growing gap between the nominal and the existential has at last to be recognized. Gradually we see that, after all, we had not arrived.

SECTION 26

"The New Testament . . . represents the dawn of cosmopolitanism as opposed to the bitter nationalism of the Pentateuch, a broadening knowledge of the world of concrete particulars that begins to be able to accommodate universalism, the concept of a single mankind."

The transition from religious nationalism to religious universalism was neither abrupt nor complete in the transition from the Old Testament to the New, or from Judaism to Christianity. Judaism has come to be regarded as a universal religion today by some if not all Jewish authorities.[49] The record of what Jesus said and did in the gospels, on the other hand, is not one of unmixed universalism. His religion, as he made clear, was the Jewish religion, and he addressed himself to his fellow Jews in the context of that religion, with many of its nationalistic implications. His command to the twelve disciples in Matthew 10: 5-6 is to "go nowhere among the Gentiles, and enter no town of the Samaritans, but go rather to the lost sheep of the house of Israel." In Matthew 15:24, when the Canaanite woman asks him to heal her daughter, he replies: "I was sent only to the lost sheep of the house of Israel." He adds: "It is not fair to take the children's bread and throw it to the dogs." The woman recognizes the distinction between the chosen nation and others, saying: "Yes, Lord, yet even the dogs eat the crumbs

[49] Cf. Isidore Epstein, *Judaism*, London, 1959, Chap. 2.

that fall from their master's table." This pitiful expression finally moves Jesus to heal the woman's daughter in spite of the fact that she is a foreigner.

But this inherited nationalism was too narrow for Jesus and he repeatedly burst its bounds. The requirement for salvation, as he defined it, was not nationality but belief. In Luke 10, the lawyer who is admonished to love his neighbor as himself asks: "and who is my neighbor?" To this Jesus replies with the parable of the good Samaritan, which says in effect that a well-disposed foreigner is one's neighbor as an ill-disposed fellow countryman is not.[50]

The real break with nationalism, however, comes after Jesus and is recorded in the Acts of the Apostles. Although the teachings of Christ had been addressed primarily to the Jews, the Jews on the whole rejected them; with the consequence that his ministry, if the apostles were to carry it on at all, had to be carried on among the Gentiles. But even Peter, close as he had been to Jesus, was taken aback by the revelation in a dream that this was allowable. To the Gentiles gathered in the house of Cornelius at Caesarea Peter says: " 'You yourselves know how unlawful it is for a Jew to associate with or to visit any one of another nation; but God has shown me that I should not call any common or unclean. . . . Truly I perceive that God shows no partiality, but in every nation anyone who fears him and does what is right is acceptable to him. . . .' And the believers from among the circumcized who came with Peter were amazed because the gift of the Holy Spirit had been poured out even on the Gentiles."

"There is no distinction between Jew and Greek," Paul wrote to the Romans, "the same Lord is Lord of all and bestows his riches upon all who call upon him. For 'every one who calls upon the name of the Lord will be saved.' "

In the old days of Leviticus Yahweh had said to Moses:

---

[50] Cf. also Matthew 8: 5-13.

201

"Say to all the congregation of the people of Israel. . . . You shall not take vengeance or bear any grudge against the sons of your own people, but you shall love your neighbor as yourself." Here is wording identical with Christ's second commandment, "You shall love your neighbor as yourself." But the meaning is different, and if the lawyer had asked Yahweh, "Who is my neighbor?" he would surely have got a different answer from the one that Jesus gave. The key to the difference is in the phrase, "your own people." In Leviticus "your neighbor" means those who belong to your own nation. Christ, in one of his transcendent moments, had gone so far as to say: "You have heard that it was said 'You shall love your neighbor and hate your enemy.' But I say to you, love your enemies and pray for those who persecute you, so that you may be sons of your Father who is in heaven; for he makes his sun rise on the evil and on the good, and sends rain on the just and on the unjust."

In a sense, Yahweh's division of mankind into mutually alien nations in the eleventh chapter of Genesis is undone, at last, in the tenth chapter of Acts. But only in a most uncertain sense, and then more in principle than in practice. It turns out not to be as easy to re-assemble mankind as it had been to scatter it in the first place. Even Jesus had been moved to say to those Jews who persecuted him that they were not children of God, under his fatherhood, but "you are of your father the devil." Here was a formula for conflict and persecution (the formula of the two species) that would not be without its exemplification in future ages.

Yahweh and Jesus are as one in admonishing men to love their own kind. The difference is in the definition of what constitutes one's own kind. "You shall not kill!" does not forbid the children of Yahweh to kill the children of Chemosh, his rival. To many Christians it has not meant that they might not kill unbelievers, the children of the devil. Christ's answer to the question, "And who is my neighbor?"

was not so comprehensive as to forbid this. Although he reduced the barrier of nationality, making it surmountable, he did not make mankind one. Perhaps, in the progressive evolution of religious thought, it was still too early for that.

SECTION 27

"I do not suppose that [progressive revelation] proceeds evenly, either on the whole or in particular media of its expression. . . . Western music, surely, began to lose its inspiration by the beginning of the nineteenth century. And it may well be that the inspiration is failing everywhere among us today."

We may judge these matters by the degree to which the limiting factor in a society's progress is that of conception or that of technique, of knowledge or of translation, of vision or of expression. The Greek sculptors of the sixth century B.C., in those archaic figures called "Apollos," were striving to realize a vision for which their technical skill was inadequate. Five centuries later, on the other hand, it was not a lack of technical skill that limited their descendants in the carving of the Laocoön or the Pergamon frieze. The culminating point of Greek sculpture (as of Greek architecture, philosophy, and drama) is in that period about the fifth century when vision and the means of expression are together at the full. The mark of the decadence that ensues is technical skill without vision, communication without a message.

For a century, now, we have ourselves been in a historic period of decadence. Our techniques have reached an advanced development, but the anti-philosophy of our age denies the real existence of any higher world to be represented by them. Our artists, with their incomparable technical skill, imitate only the imperfect material world; or they engage in abstract experiments in which lack of meaning may be the avowed meaning which they undertake to express, in which they communicate only their opinion that there is nothing to communicate. Composers produce music that is technically ingenious in terms of experimental combinations of sound, so that a trained musician may find recreation in reading their scores; but performance is without purpose, or its purpose is sensation rather than expression. Philosophy pursues an epistemology that leads to the negation of meaning. Science pursues practical ends, and the objective of politics is not "the good life" but "the more abundant life" in material terms.

The meaningfulness of lack of meaning is what recently made it possible for a painting by a chimpanzee, included in an exhibit of abstract art, to be admired by critics who had not been informed of its origin.

A similar case occurred on June 5, 1961, when the British Broadcasting Company, as a hoax, broadcast a performance of what they claimed to be an *avant-garde* composition called "Mobile for Tape and Percussion" by a Polish composer named "Piotr Zak." Miss Susan Bradshaw of the B.B.C.'s music division later revealed what the performance consisted of. "We dragged together all the instruments we could find," she said, "and went around the studio banging them." Taking this as the performance of a serious work, the music critic of the London *Times* wrote: "It was certainly difficult to grasp more than the music's broad outlines, partly because of the high proportion of unpitched sounds and partly because of their extreme diversity."[51]

When the meaningfulness of meaninglessness becomes the theme of serious art or music, it becomes difficult to distinguish such art or music from what represents a meaningless meaninglessness.[52]

2. "... *we are ahead of where we were three thousand years ago.*"

---

[51] Reported in the International Edition of *The New York Times*, August 2, 1961.
[52] See Two, 4, 3.

204

During the heat and bitterness of World War II a Roosevelt, representing the common mind, could condemn a nation collectively and advocate that, once defeated, it be held in bondage. But when the Germans were at last defeated in fact, and when our occupying forces entered Germany, there was no thought of doing what Joshua had done at Jericho. Then we recognized the Germans for what they were. We recognized them as our fellow men, and we concluded by transferring the onus of guilt from the nation to individuals, who were tried and sentenced in accordance with relatively humane and civilized procedures. One cannot imagine the Nüremberg trials in the setting of the Pentateuch.

3. *"Perhaps we shall go on ... to ... an apotheosis beyond our present conception."*

Justice Oliver Wendell Holmes once said: "I think it not improbable that man, like the grub that prepares a chamber for the winged thing it never has seen but is to be, that man may have cosmic destinies that he does not understand."[53]

SECTION 28

1. *"The idea of the United States of America, initially taking the form of words and other symbols, moves them to think of themselves as members of an American community that has its own propriety; it moves them to conform to the principles, the laws, and the other nominal particulars of the idea; and it moves them to press such conformity upon their neighbors."*

A simple illustration may be useful.

If I should suddenly give up my American citizenship and acquire British citizenship—if I should cease calling myself an American and should call myself an Englishman instead— then I would feel it proper to stop spelling "color" as I had

[53] Speech delivered in New York City, February 15, 1913; in Hicks, *Famous Speeches by Eminent American Statesmen*, St. Paul, 1929, p. 417.

up to that point and to begin spelling it "colour" instead; I should feel it proper to change from "check" to "cheque," etc. I should conform to a new and different idea of propriety.

2. *"These, then, are the terms in which we must attempt to understand the world of nation-states in which we live."*

One who has been close to the practice of politics for some years, who has become an academic student of politics, and who at last finds himself teaching politics, is moved to doubt that politics can be understood outside the framework provided by a philosophy of duality, whether consciously held or unconsciously assumed. If the terms of such a philosophy could be consciously accepted and taught as a matter of course in our universities, fundamental frustrations in the present attempts to explain politics (as in attempts to explain other things as well) would give way. Then a major portion of the political phenomena which we undertake to study would become understandable.

SECTION 29

1. *"In the Christian tradition, born at a time when the Roman Empire was disintegrating in a welter of sordidness, the state was essentially evil; and until the French Revolution there was little disposition to idealize it."*

Thomas Aquinas made the universal empire, in its dual character of spiritual and temporal, part of an ideal model for the organization of mankind; and the later apologists for the theory of divine right did not denigrate the dynastic state that was based on it. In both cases, however, as in Plato and Aristotle, the good of individual men as such is thought to require the political organization that is advocated. Hobbes justified the absolutist state only as a lesser evil, the alternative being that condition in which every individual is at war with every other, so that his life is "solitary, poor, nasty, brutish, and short." Rousseau, not distinguishing the state from the community, is the first to make it an end in itself to which the individual sacrifices his own particular ends. He is followed by the nineteenth-century nationalists—typified by Hegel and Mazzini—to whom the state is an ideal before which the individual must utterly abnegate himself and all that is his.

This idealization of the state belongs to the Jacobin tradition. The contrasting liberal tradition, harking back to early Christianity, is represented by the following passage from Thomas Paine's *Common Sense*, published in January 1776:

"Society in every state is a blessing, but government even in its best state is but a necessary evil; in its worst state an intolerable one; for when we suffer, or are exposed to the same miseries *by a government*, which we might expect in a country *without government*, our calamity is heightened by reflecting that we furnish the means by which we suffer. Government, like dress, is the badge of lost innocence; the palaces of kings are built on the ruins of the bowers of paradise. For were the impulses of conscience clear, uniform, and irresistibly obeyed, man would need no other lawgiver; but that not being the case, he finds it necessary to surrender up a part of his property to furnish means for the protection of the rest; and this he is induced to do by the same prudence which in every other case, advises him out of two evils to choose the least. *Wherefore* security being the true design and end of government, it unanswerably follows, that whatever *form* there appears most likely to ensure it to us, with the least expence and greatest benefit, is preferable to all others."[54]

2. *"Words like this [i.e., "independence," "freedom," "self-determination," etc.] tend to take on a life of their own and an intrinsic virtue, for us men, apart from any specific meaning."*

[54] Doubleday Dolphin edition, 1961, set from a facsimile of the original edition of January 10, 1776, p. 13.

The rhetorical use of these terms often tends to obscure or confuse any technical meaning they may have. The Governor of the State of Arkansas, for example, commonly refers to it, in his public declarations, as "the sovereign State of Arkansas." Words may thus have a magic property that has nothing to do with precise meaning. The citizens of Indiana proudly proclaim that theirs is "the hoosier state," though few if any know what "hoosier" means.

SECTION 30

"Each of the moral persons on the international scene equals every other as one equals one."

It is immaterial that the United States consists of some 180 million particles while Honduras consists of only 1.8 million. The United States is one person with one will; Honduras is one person with one will. One equals one. It would be unfair if the will of the United States should be assigned greater weight than the will of Honduras simply because the United States was bigger.

Some would say that, in principle, a Honduran has one hundred times the voting power of a citizen of the United States in the General Assembly of the United Nations, since the vote of the United States represents a hundred persons for every one person that the vote of Honduras represents (assuming that it does represent the Honduran people). But this view could be held only by those who thought of the individual rather than the corporate person as the basic unit. That seems to be the case with Mr. E. H. Carr. Discussing the designs for a postwar international organization that were being formulated during World War II, he wrote: "What we are concerned to bring about is not the putting of Albania on an equal footing with China and Brazil, but the putting of the individual Albanian on an equal footing, in

208

respect of personal rights and opportunities, with the individual Chinese or the individual Brazilian."[55]

SECTION 31

"It is well known that a good many people in central Europe after 1919 regretted the national freedom which had liberated them from the Hapsburg empire. The assumption that ordinary men and women gladly accept loss of their means of livelihood or of their personal liberties as the price of the freedom of their nation will be readily made only by those who have not suffered the experience."[56]

SECTION 33

1. "... the Confederation, in accordance with Swiss neutrality, belongs to nothing, not even the United Nations."

Switzerland does belong to organizations for international cooperation in other than political matters, like the Universal Postal Union. It has now become a member, as well, of the Organization for European Economic Cooperation, which also is not organized for political purposes but has possible political implications.

2. My Valaisian has been taught to celebrate as a national holiday the anniversary of the day in 1291 when the three forest cantons of Uri, Schwyz, and Unterwalden joined, as he believes, to found Switzerland. This is an example of the element of legend that is compounded with fact for nationalistic purposes. What the three states did in 1291 was to rebel against the Holy Roman Emperor, Rudolf von Hapsburg, and form a perpetual league against him. Other mountain states joined this league in the course of time. What was an alliance of independent states to begin with grew into a confederation, the independence of whose members was

[55] Nationalism and After, London, 1945, p. 43.
[56] Ibid., p. 42.

recognized after the defeat of the Emperor Maximilian in 1499, when they were released from the imperial tax. The confederated states engaged in war against each other during the religious strife of the sixteenth century but ended by renewing their accord. The European powers, by the Peace of Westphalia in 1648, recognized the independence from the empire of these states, or this confederation. But one can hardly say that there is such a thing, yet, as Swiss history based on the existence of a Switzerland. One has, instead, local histories: what happened in Luzern or Zürich, in Basel or Schaffhausen.

In 1798 the French revolutionary armies seized this constellation of states and decreed it to be "the Helvetic Republic," which was "one and indivisible," under the control of France. In the general restoration of 1815, however, Swiss independence was restored and the hitherto independent republics of Valais, Neuchâtel, and Geneva (an ancient city-state) added to the group. The members of this confederation split on the religious issue in 1847 and fell into mutual warfare. It was in the conclusion of this strife that what had been a confederation of independent states officially became, under the constitution that still prevails, one federal state. 1848 might serve as well as 1291 for the birthday of Switzerland, if the need of antiquity were to be overlooked.

The confusion of vocabulary and concepts in this history is instructive. Throughout most of it we can hardly say whether we are dealing with one or many entities, with a league of independent states, a confederation of independent states, a federal union, or a nation-state. The history is that of a slow and frequently interrupted tendency of more-or-less independent communities to coalesce, and no man can say when the process is complete or whether it has been completed even today. Legend simplifies all by adopting August 1, 1291, as the birthday of Switzerland.

3. Because nominal situations make a greater impact on

our minds than real situations, what shows up on maps of the earth may be more important than the reality it pretends to represent.

In the 1950's, with the rapid dissolution of the British and French colonial empires, there was a spate of interest and concern over an entity called Africa. Something known as African nationalism began to grow apace, and with it the Problem of Africa, the Question of Africa's Future, and so forth.

But nobody has ever seen Africa as an entity. Even those who live there cannot actually see it as that shape so familiar to us from the maps of the world. It is only from the maps that we know of it as a distinct and coherent entity, and on this point the maps are uniformly clear. Africa has as good an outline as Switzerland.

In point of fact, however, the maps are mistaken. An ocean separates the northern part of what we call Africa—the Mediterranean littoral and its hinterland—from the central and tropical area that we also comprehend by the term. If this were an ocean of water, like the Mediterranean, the map would show that there were separate entities here, for the convention of the map-makers is to distinguish the wet oceans by coloring them blue. Then the northern entity would appear far closer to Europe than to the southern entity. If it were part of one rather than the other it would belong to Europe. But the ocean that separates the area bordering on the Mediterranean from the continental mass to the south, the ocean which is so much broader than the Mediterranean, is an ocean of sand which we call the Sahara. Such dry oceans, although constituting more effective barriers than any wet oceans, are not distinguished on the maps from the land areas contiguous to them, and because of this what the maps show is one continent from the Mediterranean to the Cape of Good Hope. This causes us to think of Africa as an entity, to make a corporate person of it in our imaginations, and so to make possible the development of African national-ism and the Problem of African Nationalism.

This is, in fact, wide of the physical and historical reality. The ancient lands north of the Sahara are tied to Europe and quite cut off from the lands south of the Sahara (except for the thread of the Nile Valley, a connection as tenuous as that of the impassable Isthmus of Panama between North and South America). It is not only that the Mediterranean is narrower and more passable than the Sahara (wet oceans are so passable that they are commonly the basis of community among those who inhabit their shores). These Mediterranean lands are in the North Temperate Zone. Their basic popula-tion is white. Their history is the history of the Mediterranean basin. They were part of the Roman Empire for centuries. Virtually nothing in either history or geography connects them with tropical Africa south of the Sahara—except the common name "Africa," which denotes that familiar and deceptive image on the map of one coherent, uninterrupted territory separated from the rest of the world. Yet this makes all the difference because of the governing concept that it, by itself, establishes in men's minds, where the nominal is always more real than the real.

The inhabitants on both sides of the Sahara, calling them-selves African, begin to suppose that they must constitute one community. The rest of the world supposes it too.

4. The association called "the United Nations" is often regarded as the oecumenical community of mankind. We must see it in two distinct aspects: one, as a set of adminis-trative devices and procedures for the resolution of problems among nations; the other, as an abstract idea which may be-come invested with a corporate personality that makes a claim on the allegiance of men. In the first aspect it is a tool, an instrument; in the second it may come to be regarded as a good in itself, even an end in itself, just as in the extremes

of nationalism the nation-state comes to be regarded as a good and an end in itself.

Anyone who reviews the public debate about the United Nations since 1944 must be impressed by the degree to which it represents confusion between these two conceptions. From the first there have been those in the United States, for example, who have assumed that the United Nations is simply a place of public assembly, a forum, in which the nation-states uphold their respective views and interests. It has seemed only common sense to them that the United States should make the best use it can of the facilities provided by this forum to advance its own national views and interests, views and interests that are not necessarily unworthy of being advanced. On the other hand, there have been those to whom the United Nations represents a community, the widest in the concentric series, to which the member nations should subordinate themselves and to which men should transfer their allegiance. In this latter view the United Nations is a corporate person opposed to nationalism and to national interests, the sacrifice of which it demands of its votaries. Consequently, to use the General Assembly as merely a forum in which to pursue the national interest is improper.

In American constitutional theory the Senate as a body, while made up of men who represent the component states, stands for the whole national interest as against the partial interests of any of those states. It would be considered improper for any senator to place his state's interest ahead of the national interest where there was an issue between the two. Those who regard the United Nations as a community with a superior claim to allegiance take the same view of any tendency to regard it as nothing more than an arena in which international disagreements are resolved.

The question whether the United Nations is an arena or a corporate person with a will of its own is not primarily a question of fact. It is a question of the validity of abstractions that can never be altogether valid, and it is also a question of what fictions we ought to adopt in order to meet the dire necessity of making human society work.

5. In Two, 8, 2, having made a logical connection between the doctrine of sovereign equality and that extreme of nationalism which regards the nation-state as the basic unit of society, I cited the Charter of the United Nations as an ultimate expression of nationalism because it was based on that doctrine. This assumed the view of the United Nations as an arena rather than as a corporate person in itself. In other respects, as well, it may have been more logical than just. The critical reader may have observed to himself already that the fifty non-sovereign American states are equally represented in the Senate of the United States, or that the twenty-two Swiss cantons are equally represented in the Council of States at Berne, just as the hundred or more members of the United Nations are equally represented in the General Assembly. If the measurable inequalities among the American states or among the Swiss cantons are not as great in their extremes as among the United Nations, they are nevertheless considerable. Alaska has a population of 129,000, New York a population of 17 million; Rhode Island has an area of 1,214 and Alaska an area of 590,884 square miles; the Canton of Zürich has a population of 842,000, that of Schwyz a population of 73,200; Zug has an area of ninety-three and Grisons an area of 2,746 square miles. The logical basis of their equal representation is that each state or canton is a single corporate person with a single will, each equalling each as one equals one.

In both cases, however, this arrangement is anachronistic. It is an arrangement that, once logical in terms of sovereignty, has outstripped its logic, leaving it behind on the roadway of history. When the original thirteen American states allied themselves to make joint cause against England they did so as sovereign equals. The association among the Swiss cantons for common defense was also, in its origin, an association among sovereign equals. However, as the idea that the larger federal community was a single person with a single will became established, the pressure of that idea began to obliterate the original distinctions of what we may call personality and will among the component states.

Pennsylvania, for example, was originally founded by William Penn as a commonwealth embodying the Quaker idea of society, of human propriety. This gave it a particular distinction at the outset. But all this has faded, and today's traveler would be hard put to find significant differences between Pennsylvania and neighboring states. They have all become American, parts of the larger corporate person. Geneva in the sixteenth century, under the government of Calvin, gave an impression of distinct personality and will that has faded from this ancient center of the Protestant Reformation, now become, like Switzerland as a whole, almost half Roman Catholic. Today the Senate of the United States and the Swiss Council of States no longer represent an existing logic; but they do represent workability, and that is their justification.

6. We have twenty-four centuries of experience since Plato and Aristotle to keep us from falling into their error, which was to assume that the political pattern of their time and place, represented by the city-state, was an established and enduring pattern. City-states did not disappear with the rise of the Roman Empire, they were still not uncommon in the nineteenth century, and we have San Marino with us, still, today. But other forms of political organization came to predominate: first the universal empire and then the nation-state. There is reason to speculate that, by the middle of the twentieth century, the nation-state may be outliving, if not its workability, then at least its utility; if not in the world at large, then at least in the European world.

The unworkability of a disunited Western Europe was

patent in the years following the Second World War. With economic collapse and chaos imminent in 1947 and 1948, the United States, across the Atlantic, found that it could not effectively come to the rescue of the nation-states separately, with the result that its operations under the Marshall Plan became contingent on the creation of the Organization of European Economic Cooperation, comprising sixteen nation-states. The project of a Western European Union led, about the same time, to the conclusion of a treaty of collective military, economic, and social cooperation among Western European states at Brussels. In 1949 the Council of Europe was established, its capital at Strasbourg, with a council of ministers and a consultative assembly. In 1952 the European Coal and Steel Community came into being. In 1953 the Scandinavian countries joined in a Nordic Council. In 1959 six other European countries joined to establish a "Common Market," undertaking to live together within a common tariff-wall. Not only in Europe, but all over the free world, the menace of the Communist empires prompted the formation of organizations for common defense or for cooperation in various social and economic endeavors.

No one can say whether all this means much or little. The historical importance of events is a function of what follows from them over the decades and the centuries. To those who survey the scene of their own present, events are like innumerable seeds scattered over the countryside. Few will germinate and fewer grow to maturity. No one can say which are the seeds of the future. When the three forest states came together in 1291 to join hands against Rudolf von Hapsburg no one could have foreseen Switzerland; and surely no one would have believed that the anniversary of this move, directed only at an immediate threat, would be celebrated by five million people as the birthday of a nation some seven centuries later. If we could go back to that day we might observe innumerable events, seemingly more portentous, that have been forgotten today because they happen not to have had historic sequels.

It is idle to think that the Council of Europe, the North Atlantic Treaty Organization, the Organization of American States, or the United Nations Organization is the beginning of a vast future. It is not idle to think that one or another of them might be. The process of evolution continues, requiring ever more widespread organization of human society. The autonomous city-state is obsolete today by force of developing circumstances, circumstances that appear to be making the autonomous nation-state obsolete as well. Anyone who travels on the highways of Europe or shops in its markets can see how insufficient the nation-state has become by itself. On the highways he may cross several national boundaries in a day; in the markets he finds that even the staple food-products come from all over the map, and that any piece of machinery is likely to be assembled from parts made in several countries. Europe has one telephone network, one telegraph network, one hydroelectric network, one railway network, and one network of airlines that is part of a network embracing the world. Anyone who thinks about the problems of military defense can see the compulsion that they alone put on the European nation-states to associate. And what is true for Europe is only less true for the United States, for Canada, for the rest of the world. Consequently, among the possibilities of the future may be a gradual if hesitant coalescence of nation-states, like the coalescence of the thirteen American colonies or the Swiss cantons. The day may come when, like Pennsylvania or the Valais, their identity as prime and sovereign corporate persons has faded away.

It may be that the nation-states of Europe, so conspicuously shrunken by technological developments, will increasingly seem to their inhabitants inadequate both in the security they provide and in the majesty they represent. Dwelling under the common menace of new powers external to Europe, the idea of Europe has elements that must appeal to their allegiance. It has the majesty of a past that can, perhaps, be approached by the Chinese past but is unexcelled in all history. The claim can be made with some plausibility that civilization everywhere today is primarily European, that the elements of freedom and human dignity in whatever society they are found, as well as the elements of technology, have European roots. Europe also has a potential of power and wealth that still remains matchless. In climate and in natural resources, no other comparable area on the face of the earth is so conducive to human progress. And one can hardly doubt even today, when other peoples are making such rapid progress, that for skilled and purposeful action in support of civilization the European peoples are unsurpassed.

What Europe lacks to attract the allegiance of its inhabitants is form, the form that gives an abstract community the aspect of a corporate person to whom individual persons can pledge their loyalty. Because the United States has a President who speaks for it, the United States appears to have a personal voice and a personal will. Because the United States has physical boundaries and a capital (a capital being a head, that part of the body which controls and directs the rest) it can the more easily be conceived as a coherent personal entity. If Europe had a king or a president, a capital, a constitution, and a single color of its own on the map, one would surely find its component states losing the power to hold their own against it in the competition for men's allegiance. Only one in the series of concentric communities can possess sovereignty, and as that quality came to reside in the European community it would be lost by the component states. Only Europe would be sovereign, and sovereignty is essential to the majesty that attracts the primary allegiance of men.

Europe, then, might become, in the course of time, a successor to the European nations as Switzerland has become a successor to the Swiss cantons.

But shall we exclude Canada, the United States, the Latin American republics—all basically European countries established by Europeans overseas? Shall we exclude Australia and New Zealand? Shall we exclude the Union of South Africa? Shall we exclude Japan, a "naturalized" European state? Shall we even, in time to come, exclude the Soviet Union? And then—is it certain that India or the Philippine Republic will be less eligible than the Union of South Africa? The problem is twofold. A country as big as the United States, unlike the European countries, has not been so dwarfed by technological developments that its people feel the need of intimate identification with a larger unit at the expense of their national identity. Under present circumstances it would continue to cling to its sovereign independence. For the rest, the element of coherence tends to be lost as the area of the proposed personal entity is spread, comprehending ever greater geographical, demographic, and cultural diversity. All we are doing here, in any case, is to speculate about future developments that might go on indefinitely in an evolution without term. Switzerland began with a loose arrangement among three sovereign cantons associated by geographical propinquity, a single language, a single religion, and a single enemy. Over the centuries it came to include a greater geographical area, at least three languages, and a degree of religious diversity.

Allowing ourselves scope for speculation, we may look forward to a time when the existence of one worldwide civilization is reflected in one political organization of mankind. For, in the long view of history, the most significant fact about our present may be that, in it, a single civilization has at last succeeded in extending itself all around the globe, rapidly developing a uniform artificial environment for men everywhere. A visitor from Mars who, in the year 1500, had visited Mexico City (then called Tenochtitlan), London, Moscow, Lahore, Peking, Tokyo, and Honolulu would have seen as many separate and distinct civilizations. Visiting them again today, he would see what was essentially all one civilization.

Even though this accomplishment should be followed, in time, by the establishment of a single government for mankind, the system of concentric communities would remain— as when the city-states of Greece contained tribes and were thought of as belonging to an Hellenic nation; as when the universal Roman Empire contained nations and city-states, as among the nation-states of the West that are all members of Christendom. The several circles compete for the allegiance of the individual at the center, some becoming dominant at one time, others at another. What is subject to evolution is the relative importance of members of the concentric series.

We live in an age in which the whole complex might fall into chaos, nothing left whole, barbarian bands roving and preying amid the ruins as in tenth-century Europe. Or one power may create a universal military empire amid disorder, as Rome did. Or change may take the form of progressive developments that are relatively smooth, tending to the dominance of larger communities with the coalescence and disappearance of the smaller. Or mankind may expand into outer space, blowing apart some of the old planets to make new planets, steering them into new orbits, providing them with breathable atmosphere, and at last substituting interplanetary for international relations. Mankind may populate planets in Alpha Centauri, thereby inaugurating interstellar relations. The future may realize any of these possibilities or all, but we cannot foresee it. All we can do is attempt to understand the elements involved.

SECTION 34

I have used "state" and "community" indiscriminately, here, in referring to Rousseau's vision of the ideal monolithic

220

society. In that vision the state was not one thing and the community another. The state was purely an expression of the community as a whole. Perhaps one could say that it was the form of the community, no more to be distinguished from it than the shape of a man's body is to be distinguished from the body itself.

Both Rousseau and Marx foresaw a radical transformation of human nature. When it had taken place, all men would think alike, so that there could no longer be differences and conflicts. It was at this stage, in Marx's vision of the future, that the state would wither away.

This withering away of the state, I rather think, is implicit in Rousseau's vision as well—unless the state must remain for the conduct of foreign affairs. The *Social Contract* leaves the reader with the spectacle of a world of corporate persons, each independent, each pursuing his own self-interest. Rousseau hoped in a later essay to address himself to the problems of what, today, we call international relations, but he never got around to it. Perhaps, if he had, he would have prophesied an ultimate world (he would surely have foreseen some kind of federalism preceding it) in which all the corporate persons merged to form the single corporation of mankind under the guidance of one universal will. In fact, this possible implication of his eschatology quickly had manifestations in the early exploits of the armies of the French Revolution, which set out to "liberate" peoples beyond the borders of France and welcome them as brothers. The implication is full-blown in Marxism.

SECTION 35

1. "... *for four years* [*the United States*] *found itself fighting to subjugate the Philippine people, whom it did not want under its jurisdiction.*"

In support of this statement, see Chapters XV through XVII of my *Dream and Reality*, New York, 1959.

2. "... *the Roman Empire, which survived from generation to generation only as some ancient tree remains standing after it is dead.*"

I believe this impressive simile was first used by Spengler in his *Decline of the West*.

3. "*We ride two horses and must try to keep one foot firmly on each.*"

A classic expression of this problem in fiction is Cervantes's *Don Quixote*. Don Quixote lives only in the nominal world of mediaeval romances, being incapable of recognizing existential realities for what they are, enacting his ideas of propriety in spite of them. Sancho Panza lives only in the existential world. What gives the tale its poignancy is the reader's awareness that the foolish knight represents something more than a meaningless madness. Unlike Sancho, he has a soul. He aspires, however pitifully, to the *Logos*.

Voltaire's *Candide* is another example. Dr. Pangloss represents those frauds who make their careers as mongers of nominal ideas, using them to serve their own worldly interests. Candide, educated by Pangloss and without knowledge of the existential world to begin with, travels over two continents in an effort to find some country where existential circumstances correspond to his world of nominal ideas. In the end, he reconciles himself to living in the existential world as it is. Throughout, however, he is distinguished from the frauds and cynics who surround him by the same nobility as distinguishes Don Quixote from the lesser beings who surround him.

The theme of the two worlds, and the frustration of the one by the other, is the theme of tragedy and comedy alike, accounting for their kinship and their tendency to pass over into each other. Both deal with the same fundamental discrepancy, although each from its own point of view. In all the great tragedies the *Logos* is defeated, in the person of the hero who represents it, by the sordid existential circumstances that surround him. This is the theme of *Hamlet* and *The Brothers Karamazov*. It is the theme of *Moby Dick*.

The reason why these tragedies are uplifting rather than demoralizing is that, beneath the surface, they are affirmations rather than denials of the *Logos* in man. While it is true that, in a literal sense, the white whale defeats Ahab, in an ultimate sense it is Ahab who has triumphed by upholding the dignity of man, by showing it inextinguishable. Ahab, not the whale, stands as the model inviting imitation. And so it is with Don Quixote and Candide, with Hamlet and Dmitri Karamazov.

SECTION 36

1. *"Similarities are not as susceptible of definition as differences...."*
See Two, 5, 3.
2. The quotation of Clifton Fadiman is from his Introduction to Tolstoi's *War and Peace*, New York, 1942, p. xxix.
3. The quotation from Thucydides is from *The History of the Peloponnesian War*, R. W. Livingstone, ed., London, 1943, Book I, p. 45.

SECTION 37

1. *"In metaphysical terms it is possible to contemplate a progressive conjoining and ultimate merger of all the particles of being—of atoms to form molecules, of molecules to form organisms, of organisms to form compound bodies, and so on—until at last, in the long course of evolution, all being has become one."*
I have in mind the thesis of Teilhard de Chardin's *Le Phénomène Humain*. Here it is presented as a vision, as revelation, without supporting argument or evidence.

In Two, 2, *1*, I mention my own inclination toward

monism. In Two, 21, 2 and Two, 25, 2, I give some grounds for the inclination.

2. *"We must . . . wish to see such organization of all mankind as insures freedom of thought and expression, providing safeguards against the impositions of any absolutism."*

"The most certain test by which we judge whether a country is really free," Lord Acton wrote, "is the amount of security enjoyed by minorities."[57]

[57] Essay on "The History of Freedom in Antiquity," in *Essays on Freedom and Power*, Boston, 1949, p. 33.

224

INDEX

This is not a reference book and cannot be made to serve as such. The historical figures and events mentioned in it are mentioned to illustrate ulterior points rather than for their own sake. The following index has been supplied, nevertheless, in the thought that the reader who wishes to return to any passage already read will find that it offers him a short-cut.

The few terms of art that have an important and specialized significance for the philosophy here expounded will be found in the chart on page 127. They are all defined, or their meaning is made clear, in the first twenty-six pages of the Text.